WHAT OTHERS HAVE TO SAY . . .

SO-AYX-048

"*SAGE* provides a valuable guide for work with special needs adolescents. The 'Goals' for change and the prescriptive 'Objectives' are quite helpful and relevant to the work of educators and counselors. *SAGE* is both a practical and convenient resource which suggests many creative activities designed to promote growth and change."
>—Andrew Pollock, M.Ed., Program Director,
>Northampton Center for Children & Families
>Massachusetts

"As a counselor to children in grades 7 and 8 and their families, I found Dr. Kehayan's book a much-needed guide for parents and educators in terms of practical suggestions...a book of 'pure gold' for my professional library!"
>—Mr. Howard Harrison, M.A., House Counselor
>Scarsdale Public Schools, N.Y.

"Dr. Kehayan's clearly-written, practical book will assist teachers and counselors — and hopefully administrators — in working with adolescents toward self-possession and purpose. It engages the teacher as well as the student. It provides guidance and allows for personal style."
>—Robert Campbell, Associate Professor
>Fairleigh Dickinson University

"Dr. Kehayan has developed an excellent and practical resource from his rich background of clinical psychological skills and his extensive daily experience in relating to teacher and pupil needs. I have no doubt that the use of *SAGE* will greatly increase teachers' awareness of how to assess and to modify their pupil's behavior."
>—Dr. Zeborah Schacter, Associate Professor
>College of the City of New York

"As a school psychologist faced with the challenges of promoting personal growth in special education pupils, I have found this book enormously helpful. It has helped us focus on specific needs of handicapped children while facilitating compliance with our legal guidelines."
>—John A. Colise, M.A.
>School Psychologist

"I find *SAGE* helpful in many ways. The various activities provide students with the opportunity to develop affectively with insight into themselves. It also allows a chance for mutual growth and respect without the pressure of an authority figure judging performance. I feel the program has fostered close relationships with my students in an unforced spirit."
>—Donna Feitelbaum
>Special Educator

SAGE
SELF-AWARENESS
GROWTH EXPERIENCES

SAGE
SELF-AWARENESS
GROWTH EXPERIENCES

by V. Alex Kehayan, Ed.D.

Foreword by Barbara B. Varenhorst

REVISED / UPDATED

Jalmar Press
Rolling Hills Estates, California 90274

SAGE
Self Awareness Growth Experiences
Strategies That Promote Positive Self-Esteem for Grades 7-12

Copyright © 1990 by V. Alex Kehayan

All rights reserved. No part of this book may be reproduced by any mechanical, photographic, or electronic process, or in the form of a phonographic recording, nor may it be stored in a retrieval system, transmitted or otherwise copied for public or private use without the written permission of the publisher except as indicated on individual pages. Requests for permission should be addressed to:

Jalmar Press
Permissions Dept.
45 Hitching Post Drive, Bldg. 2
Rolling Hills Estates, CA 90274
(310) 547-1240 FAX: (310) 547-1644

20+ YEARS
AWARD WINNING
PUBLISHER
ʃ

Published by Jalmar Press

SAGE
Self Awareness Growth Experiences
Strategies That Promote Positive Self-Esteem for Grades 7-12

Written by: V. Alex Kehayan, Ed. D.
Cover design: Highpoint Type and Graphics
Photographs: Victor Fiorino and V. Alex Kehayan

ISBN: 0-915190-61-3
Library of Congress Catalog Card Number: 89-84063
Printed in the United States of America

10 9 8 7 6 5 4 3
First Edition printing. Revised and updated in 1990.

This book is dedicated to my wife,
CAROLYN,
whose sensitivity and love for
children have inspired me.

ACKNOWLEDGMENTS

I am deeply indebted to the large group of colleagues and friends who contributed toward the ideas, materials, and approaches found in *SAGE*. Many of the exercises and strategies have been passed on through the years by word of mouth, or their originators have remained anonymous. Every effort was made to locate and acknowledge the creators of exercises in this book.

Special thanks are extended to Dr. Alan Sugarman, superintendent of schools; Dr. Zelick Block, director of special education; and Dr. Val Karan, school psychologist. They have given their unselfish support and made it possible to field-test many of these approaches in the Fort Lee (New Jersey) public schools.

My appreciation is also extended to the many creative professionals who field-tested the strategies and activities, offered their expertise, and extended themselves to revise and improve the materials in the resource guide. Among the many were Carolyn Kehayan, Jill Kedersha, Donna Feitelbaum, Peter Wolf, Eileen Garner, Michael Villano, James Warnke, and Andy Fineman. Of course, *SAGE* could not have been written without the valuable feedback and thoughtfulness of the students who put life into the process.

TRIBUTE

I would like to pay special tribute to the philosophical and social pioneers who laid the foundations to make these approaches possible, including John Dewey, Albert Bandura, Abraham Maslow, Fritz Perls, and Carl Rogers.

Finally, I wish to thank all the technicians, typists, and editors, who put the process on paper and gave it more coherence. They are Dot Burland, Rose Caruso, Katherine Balik, and the staff of Jalmar Press.

TABLE OF CONTENTS

FOREWORD

It has been said that we now know enough about how children and youth grow and develop, and enough about the science and methods of providing for healthy growth — but no one is benefiting from this knowledge because we are not putting the two together to effectively solve problems or promote human growth. This baffling phenomenon may be due to a number of reasons. Anyone who has worked with youth is aware of the overwhelming number of curricula, programs, products, books, magazines, audio and video cassettes that are on the market today in the area of human development.

Where does one start to choose what should be used? How does one evaluate what at times appears to be an overlap and repetition of ideas, techniques, and intervention activities? Many address only specific areas of development, such as communication skills, interpersonal relationships, self-awareness and self-esteem, for a specific age group. How does one sort through to find what is unique about these resources for use on a broader scale with different goals and purposes? This "wealth" of resources with no guide to integrating them, may be one of the major barriers to bridging the gap between needs and services that now seems to exist.

Alex Kehayan has taken a significant step in filling this abyss with *SAGE*. Focused on eight basic goals of adolescent human growth, it offers a wide variety of strategies, which can be used in many ways to promote positive behavior in youth, grades 7-12. For each broad goal, specific objectives have been defined, with clearly described strategies for reaching the objective, most of which Dr. Kehayan and his wife have developed or modified, based on ideas of other teachers or authors. However, Dr. Kehayan has also provided the valuable resource of cross-referenced resource activities drawn from this wealth of material to select strategies and activities he feels will be useful in accomplishing the objectives. In so doing, he has helped to sort out what is available in a logical fashion, and also helpfully provided the titles and addresses of where these materials can be obtained. By virtue of this, *SAGE* is a practical catalog of learning strategies in personal and social interaction education.

I found the range and flexibility of the strategies particularly appealing. Many published materials are limited because they are geared to a specific age population, or assume that students all begin at the same level of need or skill. *SAGE* indicates strategies appropriate for different age groups and needs, suggesting that a needs assessment is an important initial step in the teaching process. Examples of methods and instruments for doing this are included.

The learning activities also are varied in terms of learning styles. These include a rich mixture of experiential, paper-pencil, group and individual activities, as well as hands on and private reflection exercises. This combination not only allows for varying interests and aptitudes, but also provides flexibility of choice in terms of an instructor's teaching methods and style.

In an age when society says it is concerned about the enormous personal problems of youth, while factions duel over the issues of academic versus affective education, *SAGE* offers ways that the two can be integrated. Frequent suggestions are sprinkled throughout the book indicating how a strategy can be used as an academic assignment. Incorporated in this way, personal growth does not have to be taught as a separate course, but as an integrated part of learning that makes academic subjects relevant to a young person's daily life. Consequently, both the learning and the life are enriched.

I am grateful for what the author has given us. Those of us who work in the field of adolescent Peer Counseling will find this a valuable resource that we will turn to in many aspects of our work.

Barbara B. Varenhorst, Ph.D.
Palo Alto, California
Founder of the Palo Alto Peer Counseling Program
Counseling Psychologist

PREFACE

It is hard to believe six years have passed since the first edition of *SAGE*. When Brad Winch, my publisher, called to advise me of his plans to produce the second edition, I was a first taken by surprise. Upon reflecting and gathering my resources, I discovered that I had a hard disk packed with new materials field-tested throughout the past six years at schools, retreats, conventions, and training sessions for professionals and peer leaders.

Since the first edition, I have been privileged to meet some truly extraordinary people who care deeply about others. A dear friend of mine, Jim Warnke, who is legally blind, asked my wife and I if we would oblige him by sharing one of our skills — mountaineering. He wanted us to guide him up a mountain before his progressing glaucoma prevented him from making the trip. We spent four of the most intensely fulfilling days of our lives guiding Jim and his son, David, up Mount Katahdin, the third highest peak on the East coast, a molehill by Western standards, but a personal triumph for a very courageous man.

Jim later made a major contribution to my professional and spiritual life by introducing me to the work of Milton Erickson. My wife and I took certification courses in Ericksonian principles, and I became so fascinated that I went on for advanced training. His work inspired me to change my whole approach to human relations and counseling. I found his messages clear, sensible and result oriented. Later, I went on to gain practitioner certification in Neurolinguistic Programming, a cross section of communication and personal change technology partly derived from Milton Erickson's work and developed by Richard Bandler and John Grinder.

I have continued to pursue my consultation and program development in the Peer Helping movement. With the help of my wife, my colleagues, and some truly dedicated peer leaders, I developed and field tested nine school-based prevention programs, which have been recognized for excellence by the U. S. Office of Education, Youth 2000, WWOR TV, and the National Mental Health Association. I have been fortunate to serve on the Board of Directors of the National Peer Helpers Association where I have met some truly dedicated innovators, who promote the ethic of peer support as a national movement.

Our nation has witnessed the terror of some accelerating central trends which require immediate attention if our planet is to survive. These include responsible environmental protection, educational revisions, and attention to the concerns of our youth and the moral tenor of our society. A variety of surveys have produced some startling statistics: Every 30 minutes in America, on the average, 685 youths will take drugs; 14 unmarried young women will give birth; 29 young people will attempt to take their lives; and 57 children will run away from their homes. These and other national crises make *SAGE's* goals even more relevant than in 1983.

This volume of *SAGE* embodies some of the visionary thinking of those who have influenced me over the years. It is on the cutting edge of a major educational trend which resurrects ethical and character education. Self-esteem continues to be of critical importance to our young people. The 37 new strategies and 7 new references also reflect a personal evolution which is the culmination of many training sessions, programs, and trial and error. I am grateful to the many caring and committed people for their support.

V. Alex Kehayan

INTRODUCTION

DESCRIPTION AND PURPOSE

SAGE: Self-Awareness Growth Experiences is a guide intended to facilitate the personal and social development of students in grades seven through twelve. The guide presents 126 strategies specifically designed to promote growth in the following eight goal areas:

Self-awareness

Self-esteem

Social interaction

Problem-solving and decision making

Coping ability

Ethical standards

Independent functioning

Creativity

The emerging importance of personal growth education during the 1960s and 1970s marked a significant turning point in American education. Having moved into the 1980s, we are clearly returning to the basic skills focus of the early 1950s. But the "Back to Basics" trend is now tempered with the infusion of the Humanistic methodologies of the 1960s and 1970s.*

Recent events have influenced our educational systems and caused a revamping of their mission. Critics have produced evidence that our students, emerging from schools with open classrooms and individualized education programs, lack the fundamental academic foundations necessary to cope with society's demands. This era of student rebelliousness, substance abuse, academic deficiencies, and moral entropy has also fueled the fires of criticism. Property tax reductions, shrinking enrollments, higher teacher salaries, affirmative action laws, federally mandated services for the handicapped, minimum basic standards, teacher accountability, rigorous evaluation and measurement, management by objectives, and severe budget cuts are but a few of the forces which have impinged upon the ability of the schools to deliver more services with less resources.

---

*This statement reflects the author's and publisher's commitment to the use of affectively-oriented strategies in the major curricula. A brief history of the educational trends of the 1960s and 1970s may be found in Appendix E.

1

Consequently, many of our schools have readjusted their curricula to meet mandated requirements at the expense of more experimental programs. These educational goals have generated a series of competing tasks, many of which are contradictory. Some of these paradoxical issues include independence versus conformity, self-discovery versus basic skills, cooperation versus competition, and creativity versus traditionality.

The increase in special educational services appears to have shifted the emphasis of affective approaches away from the regular students and toward the handicapped, particularly at the middle school and high school levels. This shift may be a consequence of expanding the basic skills programs and reallocating priorities. *SAGE* attempts to streamline the use of affective and behavioral approaches, clearly defining the target behaviors and their strategies. The outcome is a specified collection of emphases and approaches designed to promote broader use.

In reviewing the literature on human relations and behavioral approaches used in the schools, the author discovered three basic limitations which *SAGE* addresses:

1. A haphazard, disorganized series of behavioral and affective interventions lacking clear definition and clear goals.

2. A dearth of personal growth strategies at the middle and high school levels.

3. A lack of interventions designed to meet the current needs of students in the areas of coping, creativity, decision-making, and problem-solving.

SAGE responds to these limitations by organizing these ambiguous approaches to behavior change through categorizing strategies by specific goals and objectives. All the activities are targeted toward the middle and high school levels.

The author selected *SAGE's* eight broad goal categories to accurately reflect the needs of our youth during these uncertain times. Many school boards in our nation are being awakened to these needs. In fact, goals such as decision-making, creativity, coping, and ethical development form the core of instructional objectives currently being adopted by various school districts throughout the country. Thus, *SAGE* intends to clear the confusion and deal with the issues in an integrated, organized fashion.

The eight *goals* are cognitive, behavioral, and affective in nature. They encompass a wide scope of survival skills essential to the student populations and often neglected in the general curricula.

Within each goal are specifically defined *objectives*. These are designed to be observable guideposts marking the way toward the longterm accomplishment of the broader goal. Some of the objectives are written behaviorally, thus lending themselves to operational assessment techniques. Others are more cognitive or affective in nature.

Under each objective are the *strategies*, the individual and group techniques intended to accomplish the specific objectives. These strategies are appropriate for grades seven through twelve and include exercises and methodologies designed by this author and other professionals. *SAGE* uses both direct and indirect strategies.

Direct strategies require group or individual involvement. Many of these are designed to illustrate particular points — such as how it feels to be a scapegoat. Others promote skills (remembering names or offering supportive feedback to others.) Some single class session events also foster a deeper understanding of how people manage feelings by denying them, expressing them, or projecting them onto others. Other direct strategies require time frames extending beyond one classroom period. These include such projects as peer-support networks, experiential logs, individualized personal-growth contracts, and voluntary experiences in helping others.

Indirect strategies promote goal accomplishment without directly involving students in activities. These include activities such as inviting guest speakers into the classroom, developing pictorial profiles of outstanding students, and holding conferences with parents in order to generate problem-solving approaches to negative behaviors.

Both direct and indirect strategies are relevant to the specific objectives and can be used with exceptional students, counseling groups, and a variety of mainstream subjects. While the strategies are listed under specific objectives, many of them have wider applications. Appendix D includes a listing of additional uses for the strategies.

The Resource Activities are specific exercises from sources other than this volume. These activities can be found in the publications listed in Appendix B, pages 167-170. Like the strategies, they are designed to help students accomplish the objectives and, ultimately, the goals. Most of these resource activities have multiple applications and can be utilized in a 45-55 minute class period.

APPLICATION OF SAGE

The goals, objectives, and strategies in *SAGE* are intended to guide educators who occupy a wide variety of roles in diverse settings. For special education teachers, school psychologists, and learning consultants, *SAGE* can be used to develop high impact Individualized Educational Plans for the federally-mandated IEP programs for exceptional students. Family life and health education teachers may implement the strategies to help their students comprehend the intricacies of interpersonal relationships.

3

Teachers of the gifted may select goals and activities promoting problem-solving skills, stimulating curiosity and creativity, and grappling with moral and ethical issues. Group leaders, guidance counselors, and teachers of human relations classes will find *SAGE*'s techniques fit naturally into their programs with both individually and group oriented strategies.

Teachers of the core studies can utilize *SAGE*'s approaches in their classrooms. For example, a social studies class exploring community conflicts may use the strategies listed under Ethical Standards to illuminate the origins of prejudice; problem-solving strategies may serve to clarify sources of social unrest and lead to solutions.

The mathematics teacher may use exercises to promote original thinking in approaching problem-solving. For English teachers, *SAGE*'s critical commentaries, personal diaries, and logs can be used to sharpen the students' expressive writing skills.

SEQUENCE

The guide is organized by goals, with one section devoted to each. Following a discussion of each goal, objectives are delineated. Under each objective are suggested strategies for meeting the objective.

Although the goals are numbered — one through eight — there is only one area in which a sequence is suggested: Goal I to Goal II (Self-Awareness to Self-Esteem). One must be aware of one's self before one can develop self-esteem.

The objectives listed under Goal I (Self-Awareness) follow a developmental sequence which should be pursued:

1. To discover feelings and needs.

2. To demonstrate understanding of feelings and needs by describing situations which arouse such emotions as fear, anger, and joy.

3. To communicate feelings and needs effectively.

The sequence is built on the assumption that the student's path to self-awareness unfolds through discovery, understanding, and communicating with others.

After increasing self-awareness, the student goes on to use this insight to alter self-perception. Thus, Goal II (To Develop Self-Esteem) is accomplished by the following progression of objectives:

1. To refrain from self-devaluation.

2. To develop awareness of positive qualities and skills.

4

3. To adapt to new situations and join new activities.

4. To develop a repertoire of appropriate, assertive responses.

These skills build on each other. The student begins by curtailing self-depreciative behavior, and continues through the discovery of personal worth and self-confidence in various social settings. Behavior is ultimately modified to become more assertive and appropriate.

While not sequentially related, two other goals (Goal III: To Improve Social Interaction Skills; and Goal IV: To Develop Problem-Solving and Decision-Making Skills) include a sequence of objectives which build on each other. The Goal III social interaction objectives progress in the following order.

1. To relate positively to new people.

2. To participate in discussions and activities with peers.

3. To act supportively toward others.

4. To volunteer to help and seek help from others.

5. To strengthen peer relationships.

6. To sustain friendships with peers.

7. To respond positively to teachers and other authority figures.

To improve social interaction, the student must first learn to build rapport with new people, practice discussion and interaction skills, and then begin to behave supportively. The mutual support developed through helping and receiving help is an outgrowth of practice which strengthens social relationships and cements friendship bonds, thus creating lasting peer networks. A strong sense of self, combined with mutual support, lays the foundation for more appropriate relationships with authority figures.

The objectives listed under Goal IV (To Develop Problem-Solving and Decision-Making Skills) also follow a developmental course of skill acquisition.

1. To recognize when a conflict situation exists in stories, hypothetical cases, or role-playing activities.

2. To use additional information in solving problems.

3. To express alternate solutions to conflict situations.

4. To express preferences in personal choices and goals.

5

5. To explain reasons for selecting alternatives.

6. To evaluate critically the risks and consequences of making a decision.

Recognition of dilemmas is the first step to finding a solution to a problem. Gathering facts, posing alternate courses of action, and deciding which of these courses fit into the student's personal goals all contribute to the development of a rationale for making choices. Before making a decision, a student must deal with the potential results of his or her choices.

Unlike the sequential objectives presented above, the skills related to Coping, Ethics, Independent Functioning, and Creativity run parallel to each other. Since the objectives listed under these goals do not constitute prerequisites to further skill development, they are not contingent upon each other. Addressing these goals, group leaders should select those objectives which seem most appropriate to the group for individual needs.

For example, a student may have trouble resisting peer pressure but have no trouble following directions. Although these objectives, taken separately, are necessary to the development of independent functioning, they are not interdependent and should be selected as they apply to each situation.

Unlike the objectives listed above, *SAGE's* strategies are not hierarchical or progressive. However, some strategies do serve as ice-breakers or warm-ups. They may be used as introductory events to promote group interaction and cohesiveness. It is best to choose and organize strategies in accordance with the group's readiness level.

HOW TO IMPLEMENT THE PROGRAM

The flow chart shown on page 7 offers an approach to the *SAGE* program process, which is particularly applicable to the special education setting where students' individual needs define the appropriate behavioral emphasis.

ASSESS NEEDS

SELECT GOALS

SELECT OBJECTIVES

SELECT STRATEGIES

IMPLEMENT PROGRAM

Goal   Goal
  Objective   Objective
    Strategies   Strategies

Goal   Goal
  Objective   Objective
    Strategies   Strategies

Goal   Goal
  Objective   Objective
    Strategies   Strategies

REASSESS NEEDS

REFLECT

BEGIN NEW CYCLE

Listed below are the steps to guide you through the program cycle.

1. **Assess Needs.** Identify the significant personal, social, and intellectual skills of your population. To help you with needs assessment, use data from students' permanent records, individual evaluations, personal logs, sociograms, and behavioral observations. (You may wish to include your students as participants in the needs assessment process.) The following commercial instruments are assessment techniques recommended by this author:

    The Personality Inventory for Children
    Wirl, Lackar, Klinedinst, Scot & Broen, 1979

    The Self-Esteem Inventory
    Coopersmith, 1975

    Assessment of Coping Style
    Johnson & Boyd, 1980

    Behavior Rating Profile
    Brown & Hammill, 1978

    Watson-Glaser Critical Thinking Appraisal
    Watson & Glaser, 1965

    Problem-Solving Worksheet
    Lyons, 1980

    For ordering information see Appendix C.

2. **Select Goals.** If your population is a special education class, the students' handicaps are the most important determinants of goals. Take an active part in the selection process and prioritize goals based on the data generated by the assessment techniques described above.

3. **Select Objectives.** After choosing the appropriate goals, use the assessment data to break them down into specific objectives. Follow the sequence of objectives stressed in this guide under Goal I (Self-Awareness), Goal II (Self-Esteem), Goal III (Interaction Skills), and Goal IV (Problem-Solving and Decision-Making). Other objectives are not listed in any particular hierarchy and may be used as you see fit.

4. **Select Strategies.** Choose strategies and resource activities carefully. Consider your population's grade levels, intellectual capacities, and social climate. A more cohesive, verbal group will require activities that employ more self-disclosure.

    For unstable, acting-out groups, you may want to minimize risks and employ more concrete subject-oriented, non-verbal strategies and activities.

    Note: Additional strategies applicable to each objective are listed in the Appendix D.

5. **Implement Program.** A compatible, non-threatening setting is important to the group process. Make certain that the seats are comfortably arranged to allow as much eye contact as possible. Encourage interaction by asking students to talk with the group rather than to the leader. Be sure to emphasize the purpose of the group's activity, warm up the students, and become an active participant.

   Avoid calling on specific students to share personal information. This practice is often threatening and will stifle the group process. Use yourself as a positive role-model. Always be aware of your presentation style, voice tone, and non-verbal communication. Try to incorporate as much positive feedback as possible.

6. **Reassess Needs.** Assess the level of the goal and objective accomplishment of the individuals in your group at regular intervals. Many of the strategies and activities in themselves serve as assessment techniques to evaluate progress toward target behaviors. But, for more objective data, re-administer the instruments described above.

7. **Reflect.** After you have completed a cycle of selection and implementation, spend some time reflecting on your techniques of group management. Refer to David Johnson and Roger Johnson, *Learning Together and Alone*, pages 151-153, for some helpful guidelines. Assess your assets and limitations as a group leader and formulate some plans to improve your communication skills. You are now ready to begin a new cycle.

While most of the descriptions of strategies use the plural word "students" in the instructions, several can be applied to selected individuals who need to work toward specific objectives. Tailor the strategies where necessary. You will find additional procedural guidelines described at the beginning of each of the eight Goal Sections. These suggested procedures are more specifically related to each goal.

Remember, *SAGE* is intended as a guide, not a prescription. Its use generates ongoing revision and updating. Feel free to use this resource guide as a basis from which to modify, adapt, and add your own techniques to those already presented.

GATHERING FEEDBACK ON SAGE

Special education and guidance administrators who wish to evaluate the effectiveness of specific strategies used by their staff may want to utilize a feedback sheet to gain an overview of progress. Refer to the sample Feedback Sheet in Appendix A. Such a form may be distributed to staff members at regular intervals. The information gathered about the appropriateness of exercises may generate further applications to additional goals and objectives. The data may also be used to modify and update the program to meet the specific needs of your target population.

GOAL I

To Increase Self-Awareness

S ince awareness is the gateway to self-realization, this section of *SAGE: SELF-AWARENESS GROWTH EXPERIENCES* lays the groundwork for personal growth. The three objectives emphasize discovery, understanding, and communication of feelings. They are listed sequentially in accordance with their order of development. It is suggested that you use the assessment instruments listed in Appendix C to guide you in selecting the appropriate entry objective to launch your affective program.

While some strategies presented here require highly structured formats, others are more open-ended to encourage creative exploration. All strategies provide opportunities for students to disclose and reflect, to support others, to receive ideas, and to communicate personal material in an open social climate.

The brainstorming technique, applicable to group activities, is an invaluable vehicle to generate ideas, feelings and needs. This technique should also be applied to other sections of *SAGE* since it is the most important single skill in the entire repertory of personal growth activities. The conscientious use of brainstorming and adherence to its rules produce a versatile, creative, mind-expanding way of thinking. The rules should be reviewed and discussed periodically.

Rules for Brainstorming[1]

1. Strive to develop many ideas — the longer the list of ideas, the better.

2. Express no negative judgment of any idea presented.

3. Encourage zany, exaggerated ideas.

4. Expand on each other's ideas, piggy-back, elaborate whenever possible.

5. Record each idea, at least by a key word or phrase.

6. Set a brief time limit and hold strictly to it.

[1] These rules are adapted from *Values Clarification: A Handbook of Practical Strategies for Teachers and Students* by Sidney B. Simon, Leland W. Howe, and Howard Kirschenbaum (New York: Hart Publishing Co., Inc. © 1972, © 1978). A similar technique is described in *A Handbook of Structured Experiences for Human Relations*, Vol. III, by William Pfeiffer and John Jones (San Diego, Cal.: University Associates, © 1973). Adapted by permission of authors and publishers.

The basic communication guidelines and blocks listed below are also useful in facilitating group strategies.[2]

1. Practice "active listening" by giving off verbal and non-verbal signals of acknowledgment, interest, validation, and acceptance.
2. Use encouraging responses to enable the participants to continue to express and extend self-revelations.
3. Paraphrase the thoughts and feelings you receive from others. If possible, give honest reactions, and express your own viewpoints.
4. When confused about others' communication, ask questions to clarify concepts and dilemmas.
5. Avoid ordering, preaching, labeling, attempting to in-

fluence, inattentiveness, and prescriptive solutions to problems. Such reactions block avenues of personal exploration and contaminate inquiry with "borrowed values."

[2] These principles are described in *Teacher Effectiveness Training* by Thomas Gordon (New York: Peter H. Wyden, © 1974), pp. 88-89. Adapted by permission of the author and publisher.

Arrange chairs to promote eye contact without obstruction. In large groups, use concentric circles. Also use fishbowl techniques where outside group observes inner group, and then reacts to questionnaire or other feedback devise. Encourage group members to talk to the group, not to leaders. Stand near disruptive or silent members. Move isolates near friendly members. Praise all responses that are relevant. Move around the room as you present instructions. Always set the stage for each group event by getting a consensus from the group that they are ready to engage in the activity. For example, when introducing the Name Tag exercise, it might be a good idea to ask the group if they would be willing to share some personal information, and give a signal when members are ready. Such a signal might be a head nod or raised hand. Using a guided fantasy to set the mood is also helpful. For example, "Imagine that this is the first time you are meeting each other in this group. Picture what it would be like to discover some new interests and talents in other people."

Allow students to "pass" on any feelings or personal experiences that they do not wish to share with the group. Your own personal revelations can create an atmosphere more conducive to self-disclosure by other group members. Be sure to avoid issuing any grades or other judgments on these activities. By providing an open climate, teachers can help students feel free to take on new roles.

Observe the minimal cues (facial expressions, posture, changes in gestures or voice tones, etc.) shown by members as they respond. If you notice changes that signal negative internal states, ask group members to show concern by touching or moving, closer to the person in distress. It is a good idea to explore what is bothering a person privately during the break to assess the possibility of any warning signals. Always adjust your leadership to the kinds of reactions you are getting from members. For example, if you see lots of silence, you may want to change to a more up-beat activity.

Sometimes, self-exploration opens the floodgate to previously concealed, anxiety-producing emotions and behavior. Severe signs of depression, or extreme behaviors may emerge. If you notice these signals, it is a good idea to discuss what you observe, first with the particular student and then with a parent or qualified school professional. Bear in mind that it is likely that any serious emotional problems evident during the group sessions would also unfold naturally in other activities in the academic context. You need not feel that these strategies create emotional problems. Despite their therapeutic nature, none of the strategies in SAGE are inappropriate for classroom use by qualified teachers and special service professionals. They have been found to be psychologically safe and growth-provoking.

13

OBJECTIVE 1

TO DISCOVER FEELINGS AND NEEDS

STRATEGIES

1. Feelings Inventory

   To promote awareness of emotions, ask students to make a list of feelings they have experienced. Direct students to write a paragraph about one of the feelings and tell what made them feel that way. Make sure students describe the events and people who precipitate emotional reactions. Encourage sharing and discussion of feelings.

2. Name Tags[3]

   Ask students to construct personal name tags as follows:

Favorite Place		Best Day
	Name	
	Movie of My Life	
Hero		Success

   Instruct students as follows:

   > This is an exercise designed to get to know each other. On the 3 x 5 card at the top upper left corner, jot down a very special place that gives you positive feelings. It may be a place you remember from the past, or somewhere you spend time in the present. (Pause) Now, on the bottom left-hand corner,

---

[3] This strategy was developed by Joel Goodman and Frank Raimondo. Similar approaches are mentioned in *Developing Human Potential* by Robert Hawley and Isabel Hawley (Amherst, Mass.: Education Research Associates, © 1975), pp. 16-17, and in *Beginning Values Clarification* by Sidney B. Simon and Jay Clark (La Mesa, Cal.: Pennant Press, © 1972), pp. 71-74. Adapted by permission of authors and publishers.

14

write down the name of someone you admire. (Pause) Now, on the top right-hand corner, jot down what you consider to be the nicest day of your life. It may be a day of the week, a day that gave you great pleasure in the past, or it may be your idea of a good day. (Pause) Now, on the bottom right corner, jot down an event or experience in your life that you think of as a personal triumph or success. It could be learning to ride a bike, or a first date, or anything that you are proud of in the smallest or largest way. (Pause) Now, in the middle of the card, jot down the title of the movie of your life. Imagine some famous producer has asked that a film be made about you; write down the title you would choose.

Students then select partners whom they do not know. Each partner spends one minute of uninterrupted time introducing himself or herself through name tags. Each person gets one minute to question his or her partner. Partners may "pass" on any question they choose not to discuss. Students then introduce partners to another set of partners through their cards, and so on until the whole group is introduced.

3. Needs Auction[4]

Begin this event by requesting group members to brainstorm a few attributes, possessions, traits, and physical features most sought after by the participants. List these on the board and then ask the group to select ten most popular needs.

Distribute equal amounts of play money to the students and hold a mock auction during which participants have to set priorities, allocate funds, and offer bids for these desirable needs. This process will demonstrate to the group what qualities it perceives to be of high and low value. Keep a record of the selling price of each need and who bought it. Make a chart to generate discussion at the end of the auction.

Example:

Need	Price	Buyer
Love	$1,000.00	John L.
Good Looks	900.00	Peter N.
Fairness	350.00	Judy P.
Popularity	175.00	Susan J.

[4]A similar technique is found in *Human Values in the Classroom* by Robert Hawley and Isabel Hawley (New York: Hart Publishing Co., © 1975), pp. 194-197. Adapted by permission of the authors and publishers.

Ask such questions as:
- How many of these needs are already satisfied?
- Why is love so important?
- What was it like to bid on what you needed?
- How did you feel when you did or did not buy your first choice?
- How important do you think these needs will be five years from now?

Be free to share your thoughts and needs. Repeat throughout the school year and compare.

4. Personal Logos[5]

Invite students to create original personal logos of their name, initials, or insignia. Some examples that have been presented in the past include:

Teardrop Letters

Flame Letters

Heart-Shaped Logos

After students design their individual artistic logos and share them with the group, initiate discussion of how the logos reflect attitudes, personalities, moods, and backgrounds of the participants. Display the logos in the classroom.

[5]This strategy was developed by Andy Fineman, special education teacher, Fort Lee Public Schools, Fort Lee, N.J. Used by permission of the author.

5. Body-Mind-Spirit-Psyche Diamonds[6]

Make and distribute copies of the Body-Mind-Spirit-Psyche Diamond. Define each concept, giving examples to the group.

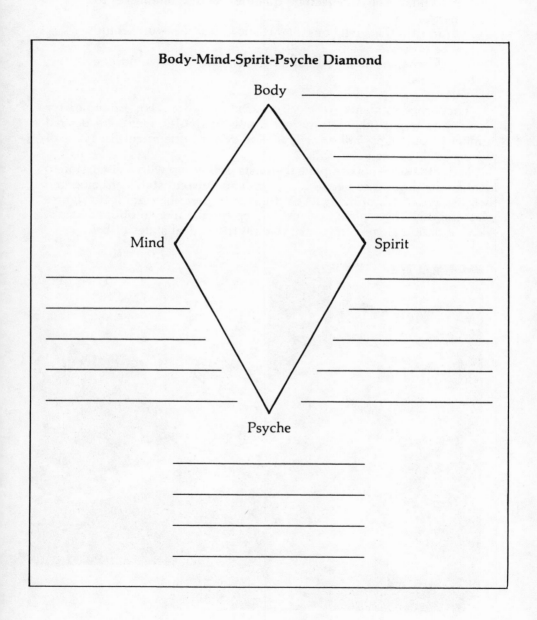

Body-Mind-Spirit-Psyche Diamond

Body

Mind

Spirit

Psyche

[6] This strategy was developed by James Warnke, M.S.W., psychotherapist, Teaneck, N.J. Adapted by permission of the author.

Ask students to list the following next to their diamonds:

Body: The physical attributes you would like to possess.

Mind: The intellectual qualities you would like to possess.

Spirit: The religious or artistic attributes you would like to possess.

Psyche: The emotional characteristics you would like to possess.

Encourage students to specify each aspiration. For example, for "Body" one might include physical fitness attributes such as a desired number of push-ups, miles, or laps. For "Mind," one might list types of writing skills or memory skills.

After the students complete their lists, follow-up with a discussion to identify the disparities between the students' current states of being and their aspired states of being. Ask students to describe significant figures who embody their physical, mental, spiritual, and emotional ideals. Also, initiate dialogue on ways to attain these ideal states of being.

6. Emotional Hieroglyphics[7]

Ask the students to imagine a feeling state they would like to express creatively. Then distribute paper, colored pencils, and or magic markers and ask the students to write a sentence describing when and where they most frequently have this feeling. Ask the group to write the sentence in such a way that the letter design reflects the feelings. For example, the sentence "I love you" might be designed in the shape of hearts. Ask each member to share their sentences and feelings.

[7]This strategy was developed by Andy Fineman, special education teacher, Fort Lee Public Schools, Fort Lee, New Jersey. Used by permission of author.

Resource Activities*	Reference Codes	Grade Levels
1. Privacy Circles	VC, pp. 183-188	7-12
2. Personal Coat of Arms	100, p. 51	7-12
3. Quickies	100, pp. 85-85	7-12
4. The Nourishing Game	100, p. 99	7-12
5. What If...?	100, p. 129	7-12
6. Friends, Lovers, and other Motivating People	UYO, pp. 46-47	7-12
7. How Did You Cope with Erikson's Eight Stages of Human Development?	UYO, pp. 51-55	9-12
8. How Shy Are You?	UYO, p. 64-65	7-12
9. Moving in Response to Group Directions	GFF, pp. 139-141	7-12
10. Making Up Games to Express Feelings	GFF, pp. 272-274	7-12
11. My Personal Goals Inventory	PE, pp. 318-333	7-12
12. Non-Verbal Concealment	DAE, pp. 67-69	7-12
13. Self-Confidence, Poise, and Self-Image	DAE, pp. 136-137	10-12
14. Moody Blues	ICE, pp. 43-44	7-12
15. Slogans That Fit	ICE, pp. 263-264	9-12
16. "Me Pictures"	TLC, p. 10	7-12

* See Appendix B.

OBJECTIVE 2

TO DEMONSTRATE UNDERSTANDINGS OF FEELINGS
BY DESCRIBING SITUATIONS WHICH AROUSE SUCH
EMOTIONS AS FEAR, ANGER, OR JOY

STRATEGIES

1. Topic Paragraphs

    Use these topics as vehicles to generate feelings about people and the emotions evoked in social and personal relationships by having students write paragraphs on topics such as the following:*

    TOPICS
    Love, Hate, and Fear
    What Is a Friend?
    Someone I Admire

After written assignments are completed, follow-up with general discussion stressing commonalities and differences. Be open and share your own reflections about the topics.

2. Twenty Questions

    Use the following survey to encourage problem posing, self-inquiry, and active goal-setting for the school year. Ask students to pick a dilemma from the questions and to log progress and changes in that particular life concern at regular intervals throughout the school year.

Twenty Questions

1. What would you like to do, have, or accomplish?

    _____

    _____

---

*Use non-verbal exercises (i.e., clapping, pantomime and thumb wrestling) as warm-up activities before assigning these paragraphs.

1. What would you like to do, have, or accomplish?

   _____

   _____

2. What would you like to do better?

   _____

   _____

3. What do you wish you had more time for? More money for?

   _____

   _____

4. What more would you like to get out of life?

   _____

   _____

5. What are your unfulfilled ambitions?

   _____

   _____

6. What angered you recently?

   _____

   _____

7. What made you tense, anxious?

   _____

   _____

8. What have you complained about?

   _____

   _____

9. What misunderstandings did you have?

   _____

   _____

10. With whom would you like to get along better?

    _____

    _____

11. What changes, for better or worse, do you sense in attitudes of others?

_____

_____

12. What would you like to get others to do?

_____

_____

13. What changes will you have to introduce?

_____

_____

14. What takes too long?

_____

_____

15. What are you wasting?

_____

_____

16. What is too complicated?

_____

_____

17. What "bottlenecks" or blocks exist in your life?

_____

_____

18. In what ways are you inefficient?

_____

_____

19. What wears you out?

_____

_____

20. What would you like to organize better?

_____

_____

3. Emotional Reactions

Ask students to collect newspaper and magazine pictures showing people expressing emotions. Encourage speculation about what feelings are shown in each picture. Have students imagine themselves in the situations depicted. Then ask each student to write a first-person monologue for one picture, explaining the circumstances for his or her emotional reaction to the situation. Follow up with a group discussion about similar feelings the students experienced in their lives.

Resource Activities*	Reference Codes	Grade Levels
1. Killer Statements and Gestures	100, pp. 67-68	7-12
2. Quickies	100, pp. 85-87	7-12
3. The Nourishing Game	100, p. 99	7-12
4. Frustration Is...	NM, pp. 19-24	9-12
5. One Possible Cause	AB, pp. 15-19	7-12
6. Common Reactions to Frustration	AB, pp. 23-27	7-12
7. Grammar	CVSM, p. 48	7-12
8. Identifying Human Needs	UYO, pp. 44-45	9-12
9. Moving in Response to Group Directions	GFF, pp. 139-141	7-12
10. Making Up Games to Express Feelings	GFF, pp. 272-274	7-12
11. Moody Blues	ICE, pp. 43-44	7-12
12. Millionaire	TLC, p. 11	7-12

*See Appendix B.

OBJECTIVE 3

TO COMMUNICATE FEELINGS, IDEAS, AND NEEDS MORE EFFECTIVELY

STRATEGIES

1. Non-Verbal Pantomime

   Hold a discussion about ways people communicate non-verbally (gestures, facial expressions, posture). Ask members of the group to act out and the remainder to guess a non-verbal message. For example, a student may act out a message in pantomime such as "Be careful!" The rest should then guess the meaning and suggest ways in which to respond most positively to non-verbal communication.

2. Para-Verbal Exercise

Encourage students to practice and refine communication skills by heightening awareness of their para-verbal messages. Have students say, "Hello" or "Come here" in different ways, using different tones and gestures. Ask students to guess the contradictory messages implied by para-verbal cues. Encourage lots of exaggeration. Facilitate a discussion on the ways in which we often project double messages in our statements.

As a follow-up, have students write a short play portraying characters using para-verbal messages. Have students jot down the implied message beneath each character's line.

3. Autobiography

Ask students to write a short autobiographical paragraph. Encourage volunteers to share their paragraphs with the group.

Ask students to respond to each other's paragraphs with the statement, "I like the part...because..."

4. Feeling Sounds[8]

To provide a non-threatening vehicle for students to discover their feelings, ask students to take turns making sounds that express their feelings or moods at that moment.

Encourage spontaneity and creativity. Use yourself as a role model. Students are allowed to use any sound sources they can discover.

As each group member makes a sound, ask the others to guess the reflected feeling. Then, encourage students to explain and clarify their sounds and feelings.

---

[8]This strategy was developed by Dr. Peter Wolf, psychologist, private practice, New York, New York. Used by permission of the author.

---

5. Totem Identity Poll[9]

Ask group members to create Native American names that capture their personal qualities. Encourage each member to also make pictures or symbols that symbolize the qualities. Such names as "Raging Bull" might capture the character traits common to the creator. Hold group discussion to identify personality traits reflected by the names.

---

[9]This strategy was developed by Andy Fineman, special education teacher, Fort Lee Public Schools, Fort Lee, New Jersey. Used by permission of author.

Resource Activities*	Reference Codes	Grade Levels
1. Practice Active Listening	UYO, pp. 112-113	9-12
2. Moving in Response to Group Directions	GFF, pp. 139-141	7-12
3. Exploring Actions Using Different Attitudes	GFF, pp. 198-199	7-12
4. Action, Reaction	GFF, pp. 252-263	7-12
5. Making Up Games to Express Feelings	GFF, pp. 272-274	7-12
6. The Positive Focus Game	PE, pp. 56-60	7-12
7. Solving Human Relations Problems in the Personalized Classroom	PE, pp. 60-64	7-12
8. Hex Signs	PE, pp. 141-143	7-12
9. Stating Clear Personal Objectives	D (LG), p. 17, D, p. 7	9-12
10. Communication and Position Change	DAE, pp. 40-42	9-12
11. Para-Verbal "Harry"	DAE, pp. 45-47	7-12
12. Giving Directions and "Successful" Communication	DAE, pp. 54-55	7-12
13. Self-Confidence, Poise, and Self-Image	DAE, pp. 136-137	10-12
14. Meaningful Symbols	100, p. 63	7-8
15. Killer Statements and Gestures	100, pp. 67-68	7-12
16. Re-Entry Questions	100, pp. 72-73	7-12
17. Positive Support Techniques	100, p. 111	7-12
18. What If . . .	100, p. 129	7-12

GOAL II

To Develop
Self-Esteem

Other human beings can be the most influential agents in promoting one's self-esteem. Most of this section's approaches to developing self-esteem invoke the communication of support and concern from others. The four objectives presented in this section follow a developmental order and should be addressed sequentially. Use the self-concept assessment instruments listed in Appendix C to help you select appropriate entry objectives. The basic principles below may guide you in enhancing the self-awareness and appreciation of others.

1. Spend some time alone with the student who lacks self-confidence. Conferences that emphasize any success, no matter how small, can be supportive and transfer positive messages to be taken in by the student.

2. Get to know the student's parents, and his or her likes or dislikes. Always acknowledge the student's presence with a friendly gesture or verbal greeting. Authentic recognition of a student's contributions to the class may be very helpful in developing a sense of self-worth.

3. Use yourself as a model to demonstrate some of the vehicles used to encourage self-disclosure and initiate discussions.

4. Emphasize the positive qualities and abilities of the student. Encourage his or her responses to questions and activities in which the student shows interest or competence.

5. Urge the student to seek guidance and support from special service personnel, counseling groups, peer activities, and formal clubs in the school and community.

6. Initiate confidential discussions about the student's behavior with his or her other teachers and support service personnel. A uniform positive approach may emerge from such conferences and impact the student in a consistently supportive way.

OBJECTIVE 1

TO REFRAIN FROM SELF-DEVALUATION

STRATEGIES

1. Physical Education Improvement Chart

     Direct students to choose one or two physical education activities which offer them the potential for success. Personal Improvement Charts on each activity should be assigned and the students should record each week's successes and improvements on their charts.

     Physical Education teachers should monitor the students' progress by setting up individual monthly conferences. At the end of the school term, ribbons or awards should be presented to students who demonstrate continuous progress. Try to acknowledge as many students as possible.

2. Share a Skill

     Assign students to lead an activity, teach a lesson, demonstrate a skill, or report to the group on a personal interest such as photography, sports, or games. Elicit positive feedback from the group on its members' presentations.

     Have students construct posters or projects highlighting the major aspects of their skills. Following presentations, display all projects in the room so that the class may continue to share and learn from each other. Students may also want to run off hand-outs which summarize their presentations and suggest ways those interested might pursue this skill or interest.

3. Joining the Student

Move close to students when they express positive thoughts, articulate ideas about the subject, or otherwise show involvement in the ongoing activity. Your attention should reinforce the development of positive behaviors.

In addition to acknowledging a student in front of the class, speak privately to the student after class, saying: "Your contribution today really added a lot to the lesson"; "The class really seemed to enjoy your comment about...."; or "Your behavior in class today was outstanding. Keep up the good work!"

4. Variation on a Lyric

Ask group members to try listening to their favorite music and making up new lyrics that guide them through a difficult situation. "I'm going to make it through this mess, the way I did last time...." It sounds silly, but it will work with the more light hearted.

Resource Activities*	Reference Codes	Grade Levels
1. Success Sharing	100, p. 41	7-12
2. Success a Day (Once a Week)	100, p. 49	7-12
3. IALAC (I am Lovable and Capable)	100, pp. 91-93	7-12
4. I Don't Mean to Brag, But...	NM, p. 108	9-12
5. Self-Sabotage Role Play	DHP II, pp. 34-35	7-12
6. Look What They've Done to My Brain, Ma: An Exercise in Creativity and Self-Concept	AE, pp. 203-205	7-12
7. "I Can..." Statements	PE, pp. 87-88	7-12
8. Photographs	DAE, pp. 121-122	7-12
9. Color, Car, Character	ICE, pp. 219-220	7-10
10. "Proud Experience"	TLC, p. 15	7-12

*See Appendix B.

OBJECTIVE 2

TO DEVELOP AWARENESS OF POSITIVE QUALITIES AND SKILLS

STRATEGIES

1. Personality Collage[10]

    Use this technique to promote self-discovery.

    Ask students to create a collage depicting their own interests, feelings, ideas, and hobbies.

    Distribute 11 x 14 construction paper, scissors, paste, magazines, and felt-tip marker pens. Over a series of four periods (approximately 45 minutes each), ask the students to go through the magazines and select any pictures and words that can be used to portray themselves. Instruct the students to use markers to add words and pictures to complete their personal picture portraits.

Then request each group member to say a few words about his or her collage and elicit feedback from other members of the group on each person's profile. The teacher may also participate by creating his or her own collage and discussing it with the group members. The collages can be hung in the room or taken home by the students.

[10]A similar strategy is described in "Scissors, Glue, and English, Too," by Robert C. Hawley and Isabel L. Hawley in Independent School Bulletin, Vol. 33, No. 1 (October 1973), pp. 41-43. Adapted by permission of authors and publisher.

2. Pass a Game Along

Demonstrate to the group how to teach a game to others. Emphasize including the goals, activities, and rules. Then divide the group into pairs and direct each student to teach a game to his or her partner. Make a collection of the games used by students. Allow students to play their games during free time.

3. A Hand Silhouette[11]

Divide the group into pairs. Ask partners to assist each other in tracing one hand of each person on a piece of white construction paper.

Each student then takes a few minutes to study his or her own hand and to list under the silhouette:

1. Distinctive features that make it my own hand.
2. What I like about my hand and what makes it special.
3. What my hand can do well.
4. How my hand can help others.
5. Any other powers that my hand has.

Divide into small groups and instruct members to introduce themselves through their hands. Facilitate a reflective discussion on the qualities symbolized by silhouettes.

[11]This strategy was developed by Steven Denes, director, Comprehensive Health Project, District Four, New York City Public Schools. Adapted by permission of the author.

4. Taking Charge

Visualize and experience a positive state when you were in charge and had it all together. Imagine yourself being in the scene and run it in slow motion with all the sights, sounds, colors, smells, and people. Think of your own special code or symbol that you can use to remind yourself to get back the power state. The symbol might be a color, name, code, or vision that ushers in the positive state you need to act effectively when under stress.

Resource Activities*	Reference Codes	Grade Levels
1. Do you Perceive Yourself as an Origin or a Pawn?	UYO, pp. 61-62	9-12
2. Affirming Yourself	UYO, pp. 85-86	9-12
3. Enhancing Your Self-Concept	UYO, pp. 90-91	9-12
4. "I Can . . ." Statements	PE, pp. 87-88	7-12
5. Values Scavenger Hunt	PE, pp. 129-131	7-12
6. Hex Signs	PE, pp. 141-143	7-12
7. Photographs	DAE, pp. 121-122	7-12
8. Self-Confidence, Poise, and Self-Image	DAE, pp. 136-137	10-12
9. Success Sharing	100, p. 41	7-12
10. Pride Line	100, p. 47	7-12
11. Personal Coat of Arms	100, p. 51	7-8
12. Success Symbols	100, p. 57	7-12
13. Quickies	100, pp. 85-87	7-12
14. IALAC (I Am Lovable and Capable)	100, pp. 91-93	7-12
15. Strength Bombardment	100, pp. 96-97	7-12
16. Making It Real	100, p. 102	7-8
17. Commercial for Oneself	100, p. 109	7-8
18. Distinctive Feature(I)	AG, p. 32	7-12
19. Distinctive Feature (II)	AG, p. 33	7-12
20. Finger Collage	ICE, pp. 29-30	7-12

*See Appendix B.

OBJECTIVE 3

TO ADAPT TO NEW SITUATIONS AND JOIN NEW ACTIVITIES

STRATEGIES

1. Guest Speakers

    Invite resource persons from the school or community into the group to present activities and programs available for students. Encourage group members to select activities of interest; to pursue these activities; and report back to the group on their new interests.

2. Needs-Action Stories

    Ask students to write or record stories telling about something they want to learn and how they would master it. Each member should read his or her story aloud and elicit reactions from the group. Then encourage the students to pursue these activities and report periodically to the group on their progress.

3. Experience Sheets

    Ask each student to fill out the following Experience Sheet, indicating preferred activities and hobbies. Tell members who have no current leisure time pursuits to investigate possible alternatives that might seem interesting to develop. Possibilities might include: school clubs, band, sports, collecting objects, nature activities, writing, choral groups, Boy Scouts, Sea Scouts, Civil Air Patrol, and 4-H Club.

```
┌─────────────────────────────────────────────────────────────┐
│                     Experience Sheet                        │
│                                                             │
│   Name _____ Grade _____ Date _____   │
│                                                             │
│   Area of Interest _____  │
│                                                             │
│   Type of Activity _____  │
│                                                             │
│   Others who are interested_____   │
│                                                             │
│   _____  │
│                                                             │
│   Ways to get together  _____   │
│                                                             │
│   _____  │
│                                                             │
└─────────────────────────────────────────────────────────────┘
```

Based on the Experience Sheets, assign students to small groups to develop projects with others of similar interests. Share the projects by having them presented to the entire group.

Resource Activities*	Reference Codes	Grade Levels
1. Goals as Understood	DHP II, p. 28	9-12
2. Moving in Response to Group Directions	GFF, pp. 139-141	7-12
3. Follow the Leader (II)	GFF, pp. 155-156	7-12
4. Trust Walk	BVC, p. 79	7-12
5. Crossword Puzzle	AG, p. 31	7-12
6. Student-Student Interaction	LTA, pp. 130-132	7-12
7. Prehistoric Animals	ICE, pp. 53-54	7-12

*See Appendix B.

OBJECTIVE 4

TO DEVELOP A REPERTOIRE OF APPROPRIATE ASSERTIVE RESPONSES

STRATEGIES

1. Student-Teacher Conferences

    Initiate individual conferences with students who appear to have difficulty asserting themselves. Encourage them to voice the needs and obstacles that affect their school performance and interpersonal relationships. Use active listening techniques to elicit appropriate assertive remarks. Be responsive to appropriate requests.

2. Coping with Others' Undesirable Behavior

Introduce this strategy by describing how we all sometimes face situations in which people behave offensively. Identify and list some behaviors that the students find provocative. Have students demonstrate and record various responses to the annoying behavior and habits of others.

Then, initiate a brainstorming activity to generate alternative non-threatening ways to help others change offensive habits. Record the appropriate assertive responses and distribute to the group.

3. What's Behind the Agressive Outbursts?[12]

The following exercise is designed to sensitize group members to the real messages behind verbal aggression.

Ask students to form groups of three. The members of each group take turns playing roles of actor and responder. The actor gives a verbal outburst and the other two members take turns responding to the outburst with an interpretation of the covert meaning. The actors then rephrase the outburst, making it an expression of the real message.

Example
Actor (to Parent):
    You always go out and leave me with some stupid adult.
Responder 1:
    You're really angry at your parents.
Responder 2:
    You feel abandoned and rejected by your parents.
Actor's rephrase:
    When you leave me, it makes me wonder whether I am important. It just isn't fair to me.

Enlist the group's aid in producing example of typical angry outbursts towards others. Role-play them, with responders interpreting intended messages.

Some examples of Outbursts:

1. Get off my back!
2. I hate your guts.
3. You're a pain in the neck.
4. Why don't you take a walk?

[12]This strategy was developed by Michael Villano, chairman, Social Studies Department, Fort Lee High School, Fort Lee, N.J. Adapted by permission of the author.

4. Confrontation Guidelines and Barriers

Ask group members to use these guidelines to practice effective confrontation skills. In the large group, request members to read each Guideline and Barrier aloud and make up an example of each. Then have them form groups of four, make up scenarios, and role play them using these skills.

Confrontation Guidelines

1. Be flexible in setting up your expectations about the outcome of the confrontation.
   "The most important thing is that he knows what an inconvenience he caused me."

2. Timing and location are critical to a successful confrontation. Privacy and easy access to each other will usually improve the impact, unless you are concerned about a physical confrontation.

3. Talk directly to the person you are confronting.
   "I really need to tell you something very important."

4. Talk clearly and calmly. If the person is unable to listen, wait until he or she is in a more receptive state.

5. Always pace and match the person whom you are confronting.

6. Refer directly to the issue.
   "Remember when we were supposed to meet at Burger King last Friday?"

7. Explain how the person's behavior affected you. Use "I" messages.
   "I get furious when you keep me waiting."

8. Always listen actively to the other person's viewpoint. Put yourself in his or her shoes.

9. Ask for cooperation and openness. This will test the person's flexibility.
   "Will you hear me out?" "Would you be willing to change the way you treat me?"

10. Summarize what you need to resolve the problem.
    "I need to know that you will avoid unloading your bad days on me."

Confrontation Barriers

1. Avoid setting up unrealistic expectations about the outcome of the confrontation. If you realize you can't get what you want by confronting, then try something else, like a directly stated letter.
   "He is going to pay me back all the money by tomorrow!"

2. Avoid letting your anger build up to a rage state.
   "You have gone too far this time... I've had it."

3. Avoid telling others about the upcoming confrontation. The impact will be diluted if the person hears your complaints from others.
   "You won't believe what he did. Wait till I find him."

4. Avoid confronting a person in a crowd or among his/her valued friends. It will rally defensiveness and neutralize the effect.

5. Avoid labelling the person you confront or the behavior that angered you.
   "How could you do such a dumb thing?" "You're stupid."

6. Avoid asking set-up questions.
   "Don't you have any common sense?"

7. Avoid ultimatums and threats.
   "This is the last time you will ever try that!"

8. Avoid accusations.
   "Why did you tell Judy what I said about her?"

9. Avoid why questions. They usually invite distortion or deception.
   "Why on earth did you do that?"

10. Avoid beating around the bush.
    "Some people have been saying that you really want out."

11. Avoid ordering specific resolutions to the conflict.
    "You'd better apologize to her immediately or else."

Resource Activities*	Reference Codes	Grade Levels
1. Privacy Circles	VC, pp. 183-188	7-12
2. Letters to Editor	VC, pp. 262-263	7-12
3. RDA's	VC, pp. 358-362	7-12
4. Expressing Anger	HB IV, pp. 104-106	7-12
5. Killer Statements and Gestures	100, pp. 67-68	7-12
6. Teacher Feedback	100, pp. 78-79	7-8
7. The Public Statement	100, pp. 143	7-12
8. Making Your Wants Known	100, pp. 180-181	7-12
9. Practicing Covert Rehearsal to Become More Assertive	UYO, pp. 83-84	9-12
10. Action, Reaction	GFF, pp. 262-263	7-12
11. Communication Guidelines Rank Order	HV, pp. 124-126	7-12

*See Appendix B.

GOAL III

To Improve Social Interaction Skills

Since we are all social beings, in great measure dependent upon our interactions with others, it is essential that any personal growth curriculum provide experiences designed to promote social harmony. Social Interaction is divided into seven developmental objectives which are attained sequentially. To determine appropriate entry objectives, use the observation checklists, sociograms, and self-concept scales listed in Appendix C.

The strategies in this section provide hands-on experiences stressing social interaction in a non-threatening, cooperative atmosphere. They also invite students to explore the dynamics of their own group as it gropes with issues of authority, leadership, responsibility, gender conflicts, and mutually desirable outcomes.

Leaders should make every effort to provide clear directions, time limits, and positive feedback. Leaders should also model their own interaction through open participation during the events. Negative feedback should be avoided. The flow of interaction is greatly enhanced by respecting the privacy and personal opinions of the participants. Acknowledgment of each person's contribution and persistent questioning is standard operating procedure in promoting more meaningful communication.

Seating arrangements should provide maximum visual contact between members. Use of the fishbowl techniques, in which one group surrounds another to observe the first group and comment on participation, is an excellent way to study and improve interaction. Apply this technique to strategies involving group activities throughout *SAGE*.

Role-playing is a valuable technique to promote improved social interaction. When you initiate role-plays, set the stage by describing the background of the characters and the situation. Have the characters describe their feelings. Sometimes it is useful to ask students in the audience to pick out characters, study their behavior, and then describe how their response to the situation might differ.

OBJECTIVE 1

TO RELATE POSITIVELY TO NEW PEOPLE

STRATEGIES

1. Communication Network Handout

    Ask students to write down their names, addresses, phone numbers and their best academic and social skills. Distribute this information to group members and encourage them to contact each other about homework assignments, group projects, and any other problems that arise.

2. Friendship Chart

    Ask students to dictate ideas about what a friend is. Make a list of qualitites generated by the group and hold a discussion about how those characteristics guide you to initiate new friendships.

    Example
    A friend will not hurt you. Friends trade things. A friend is someone you like and who likes you. A friend does not tell on you.

3. Welcome Letters[13]

   This strategy may be used to acquaint incoming members with the setting, routines, and expectations of the group and its leader. Ask each current member to take fifteen minutes to write a personal letter to an incoming member. The letter should include a description of the group's:

   setting

   goals

   activities

   leader

   membership

   expectations

   do's and don'ts

Ask students to conclude their letters with some brief advice to the incoming members.

   If the names and schools of incoming students are known, send the letters in advance. If incoming members are unknown, collect the letters and distribute them when the new group or class begins.

[13]This strategy was developed by Andy Fineman, special education teacher, Fort Lee High School, Fort Lee, N.J. Used by permission of the author.

4. The Elevator[14]

   Without any preparation, ask the group to move their desks to one side of the room. In the center of the room, tape a square (at least five feet square) on the floor. Tell students, "This is an elevator." Ask for one volunteer to step into the elevator. (Pause) Then ask if anyone else would like to get into the elevator. Continue asking for volunteers, one at a time, until the elevator is packed.

   Then, engage the entire group in a discussion. Stress the subtle changes observed as each person stepped into the elevator. Inquire about the students' adjustments in space and their attitude changes as the elevator was being filled. Stress significance of posturing (face-to-face or diagonal). Draw analogies between this situation and other social contexts where new groups are formed.

   Repeat this exercise at regular intervals to assess the cohesiveness of the group. Engage members in discussions of how the elevator exercise reflects the group's current level of functioning.

[14]This strategy was developed by Michael Villano, chairman, Social Studies Department, Fort Lee High School, Fort Lee, N.J. Used by permission of the author.

Resource Activities*	Reference Codes	Grade Levels
1. Trust Walk	BVC, p. 79	7-12
2. Want Ad	BVC, pp. 98-99	7-12
3. Moment of Beauty	DHP II, p. 13	7-12
4. Pipe Cleaners	DHP II, p. 14	7-12
5. Moving in Response to Group Directions	GFF, pp. 139-141	7-12
6. Follow the Leader (II)	GFF, pp. 155-156	7-12
7. Name Game	100, p. 31	
8. Biographies	PE, pp. 43-44	7-12
9. Acceptance/Rejection	DAE, pp. 142-144	10-12
10. Introducing Partners	AG, pp. 27-28	7-12
11. Portrait and Interview	AG, p. 29	7-12
12. Crossword Puzzle	AG, p. 31	7-12
13. Student-Student Interaction Game	LTA, pp. 130-132	7-12
14. Friends	TLC, p. 64	7-12
15. Life Map	ICE, pp. 93-94	7-12
16. All Tied Up	ICE, p. 211	7-12
17. Finders	ICE, pp. 235-237	7-10
18. Telegram	TLC, p. 5	7-12
19. Commonalities	TLC, p. 40	7-12
20. Prehistoric Animals	ICE, pp. 53-54	7-12

*See Appendix B.

OBJECTIVE 2

TO PARTICIPATE IN DISCUSSIONS AND ACTIVITIES WITH PEERS

STRATEGIES

1. <u>Activity Planning</u>

Have students form groups to plan an activity (i.e., art, music, class play). Let them assume responsibility for any necessary classroom adaptation. Discuss why forming groups to do certain jobs is helpful. Ask what would happen if each group member did not do his or her job, and thus evoke ways of developing responsibility and cooperation by working in groups.

2. Conversation Logs

Ask students to keep a record of their conversations with friends, employers, parents, teachers, and relatives. Have them classify the types and purposes of these conversations and to evaluate them in terms of enjoyment, satisfaction, needs fulfillment, and level of depth.

Request students to enter their comments in their logs each week, stating what they have learned about the different ways they communicate.

3. Conversation Pieces

As a means to acquaint group members with each other, ask them to bring in an object from their home that tells something about their life. Objects may be personal artworks or creations, food, music, books, or anything that has special meaning to the individual.

Spend several periods encouraging the students to explain their conversation pieces. Ask the group members to describe the significance of the objects and encourage questions.

4. Scavenger Hunt

Set up a short list of experiences, qualities, and profiles for each member to find and then report back to group in large discussion. Seekers may look for people who drink soda for breakfast, chocolaholics, iguana owners, nature lovers, etc.

Resource Activities*	Reference Codes	Grade Levels
1. Name Game	100, p. 31	7-12
2. Quickies	100, pp. 85-87	7-12
3. Trust Walk	BVC, p. 79	7-12
4. Questions to Get to Know Someone Better	DHP, pp. 15-16	7-12
5. Commonalities	DHP, p. 16	7-12
6. Bumper Stickers	DHP II, p. 10	7-12
7. What's Your Line?	DHP II, p. 10	7-12
8. Practicing Active Listening	UYO, pp. 112-113	9-12
9. Personal Message: An Audiotape Presentation	AE, pp. 37-38	10-12
10. Add a Movement, Sound or Shape	GFF, pp. 134-135	7-12
11. Moving in Response to Group Directions	GFF, pp. 139-141	7-12

Resource Activities*	Reference Codes	Grade Levels
12. Follow the Leader (II)	GFF, pp. 155-156	7-12
13. Establishing Identity (I)	GFF, pp. 235-236	7-12
14. Solving Human Relations Problems in the Personalized Classroom	PE, pp. 60-64	7-12
15. More Motions	ICE, pp. 45-46	7-10

*See Appendix B.

OBJECTIVE 3

TO ACT SUPPORTIVELY TOWARD OTHERS

STRATEGIES

1. <u>Inventories of Cooperation and Conflict</u>

    Present a list of sentences demonstrating supportive and unsupportive behavior. Select sentences from the list and engage in discussion based on group members' personal experiences. Identify the consequences of disharmony and elicit examples of ways to enhance cooperation.

    Examples:
    1. All members of the basketball team did their best to win the game.
    2. Bill keeps interrupting Tom when he tells his story.

2. <u>Cooperative Situations</u>

    Provide oral or written examples of cooperative groups in society.

    Examples:
    1. Assembly line production
    2. U.S. Senate
    3. N.A.S.A.
    4. Israeli Kibbutz

    Have students respond to your examples by identifying what types of behavior are necessary to complete each group's task. Initiate discussion explaining the rules of each group and their rationales. Encourage students to describe how they might be more helpful in their own task groups.

3. String Maze[15]

Try this experiment with the group to discover how positive and negative feedback affects learning and performance.

Tell the group they are about to participate in an experiment to see how they can influence each other's performance. Enlist one volunteer as the "performer." With a long piece of string, lay a straight line on the floor extending from one wall to the opposite wall. Instruct the performer as follows:

Your task is to keep your feet on this line as you walk from one side to the other. You will be wearing a blindfold (handkerchief or scarf). Your fellow students will be guiding you.

Ask students to form two groups. Group A is instructed to give positively toned verbal feedback as the student walks the line, i.e., "You're getting close." "You're on it." "You're doing great!"

Group B is instructed to give negatively toned verbal feedback, i.e., "You're way off." "Come on, can't you do better than that?" "You're off the mark."

Group A is located at both sides of the line-up to the mid-point. Group B is located on both sides of the second half of the line.

As the performer walks the first half of the line, Group A members speak. Group B members speak as the performer walks the second half of the line.

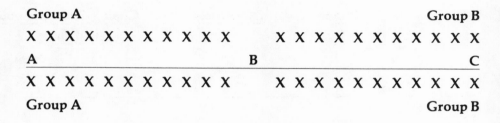

Group A   Group B

X X X X X X X X X X X   X X X X X X X X X X X X

A   B   C

X X X X X X X X X X X   X X X X X X X X X X X X

Group A   Group B

Count the number of times each foot touches the line along the first half (with verbal reinforcement), and the number of touches for the second half (with verbal punishment). Usually, the performer will score more touches from Point A to B than from Point B to C.

Tally the scores and hold a discussion about how the performer felt under both conditions, and what the observers noted about his or her behavior. Ask what it is like to receive (and to give) positive and negative feedback and how it can affect performance in other areas of life.

[15]This strategy was developed by Dr. Robert Ostermann, professor, Psychology Department, Fairleigh Dickinson University, "String Mazes" © 1978. All rights reserved. Used by permission of the author.

4. Your Support Network

Set up a peer support system to share coping strategies that might be useful to others in the group.

Ask the group to recall some situations they have been through, challenges they have overcome, and storms they have weathered. These may include going through a parental separation or divorce, losing a special friend, passing a difficult subject, making a speech, or overcoming a conflict with a friend. Ask those members willing to support others going through similar problems to share experiences and coping strategies. Distribute a Support Network Sheet, and ask members to list names, phone numbers, experiences, and coping strategies.

Photocopy the sheet and distribute to group with a follow-up instruction for the future that they find a way to share these experiences with others and report back to the group periodically. The personal support group may be used to assist members in coping with their own problems and reaching out to others.

Resource Network Sheet

Name	Phone	Experiences	Coping Strategies you will share

Permission to reprint Copyright © 1990, V. Alex Kehayan, *Self-Awareness Growth Experiences*, Jalmar Press, Rolling Hills Estates, CA.

5. Haves and Have-Nots

Divide group into two sections. One section, the **Haves**, has everything they could possibly want while the other group, the **Have-nots**, is empty. Ask the Have-nots to identify their needs in life that are important to them — physical, mental, material, spiritual. In five minutes the Have-nots must try to get as many needs as possible from the Haves without any verbal communication. The Haves may or may not decide to meet their demands.

Resource Activities*	Reference Codes	Grade Levels
1. Medical Emergency	CGG, p. 26	7-12
2. Mixed Feelings	LHT, pp. 66-77	7-12
3. Broken Squares	HB I, pp. 25-29	7-12
4. Learning Teams	DHP, pp. 73-74	7-12
5. What Do You Know? What Do You Want to Know?	DHP, p. 75	7-12
6. Personal Message: An Audiotape Presentation	AE, pp. 37-38	10-12
7. Killer Statements and Gestures	100, pp. 67-68	7-12
8. IALAC (I am Lovable and Capable)	100, pp. 91-93	7-12
9. Trust Walk	BVC, p. 79	7-12
10. Want Ad	BVC, pp. 98-99	7-12
11. Christmas Gift Giving	VC, pp. 353-355	7-12
12. Blackboard Role Play	RP, pp. 49-53	7-12
13. Mathematics	CVSM, pp. 60-65	7-12
14. Add a Movement, Sound, or Shape	GFF, pp. 134-135	7-12
15. Solving Human Relations Problems in the Personalized Classroom	PE, pp. 60-64	7-12
16. Conflict Resolution	PE, pp. 75-79	7-12
17. Group Rejection	DAE, pp. 102-106	7-12
18. Teacher Role Checklist for Cooperative Instruction	LTA, pp. 133-134	7-12

Resource Activities*	Reference Codes	Grade Levels
19. Finger Collage	ICE, pp. 29-30	7-12
20. Caterpillar Race	ICE, pp. 17-18	7-12
21. Off Your Chest	ICE, pp. 97-98	7-12
22. Style Show	TLC, p. 29	7-12
23. Feedback on Nonverbal and Verbal Behavior	DHR, pp. 35-37	10-12

*See Appendix B.

OBJECTIVE 4

TO VOLUNTEER TO HELP AND TO SEEK HELP FROM OTHERS

STRATEGIES

1. Pictures Showing Cooperative Behavior

    Ask students to select pictures from magazines that show people helping others. Discuss the possible needs and responses depicted. Encourage students to brainstorm several helpful responses for each picture. Initiate discussion of applications to group members' lives.

2. The New Student Role Play

    Engage the group in a role play entitled, "The New Student." Focus on the feelings and difficulties a new student encounters when confronted with cliques, new teachers, and school policies. Include ways the class can make him or her more comfortable.

    As a follow-up to this exercise, ask for volunteer students to form a "welcome committee." The committee will be responsible for helping new students with their lockers, schedules, classroom locations, and school procedures.

3. Helping Diary

    Ask students to keep a weekly diary entitled "Ways I Have Helped Others." Students should be encouraged to share their different approaches with peers and adults. Discuss the types of feelings experienced when reaching out to others.

4. Emergencies Unit

    Develop a four-week unit on the occurrence of emergencies (natural, personal, health, accidental) and encourage group members to research ways to react and cope. Use multi-media demonstrations, literature, and guest speakers to enhance the presentations. Initiate discussions to sensitize students to appropriate emergency behaviors. Develop a collectively designed list of appropriate helping responses.

5. Peer and Cross-Age Helping

On a voluntary basis, pair an independent with a dependent student, or older pupil with a younger pupil of the same sex. Encourage peer helper to teach a skill that the partner requires, i.e., correcting composition, factoring, map skills, etc. The helper should be patient, empathetic, and articulate. He or she should seek assistance from the instructor if necessary. Seat the pair together in a separate section of the room and monitor at regular intervals.

6. PIN — Peer Intervention Network

Select an even number of bright, unmotivated, underachieving students for this project. After obtaining approval from parents and principal, initiate an agreement with students and parents to set up a five-month Peer Intervention Network (PIN) program. The network should meet for three 45-minute sessions per week during lunch, before, or after school. Once the contract has been made, the meetings are obligatory.

Explain that the purpose of the program is to work together to improve everyone's academic performance. Describe the roles of "shadows" as helping agents, "consultants" as resources to the group, and "experts" as reformed members who have excelled in their weak areas.

Distribute PIN Fact Sheets to the group and explain the procedures and responsibilities. (See page 59 for an example of this form.) Go over the sheet and show how the group is intended as a support system. When members reach their goals, they no longer require "shadows," but become "experts" who serve as consultants to the group. Essentially, this is a reward system based on achievement. Stress the interdependence of the group and the importance of others in the process.

Here are the guidelines:
1. Every student in the group fills out a *Self-Evaluation* form to guide his or her self-reflection, determine subject areas that need attention and identify problems blocking progress (See page 61 for an example of this form.)
2. Each student serves as a "shadow" to another in the group. The shadow must meet with his or her partner, assess the target subjects to pursue, and phone the partner every night to check on his or her study progress. Shadows must report to the group at each meeting and discuss the progress of his or her partner. A *Plan of Action* form is used to decide on the areas that need improvement, and to monitor progress. (See page 62 for an example of this form.)
3. Use the first week's sessions to set the ground rules and establish plans of action. Ask each student to list his or her best subjects and phone number on a sheet of paper. Distribute this list of consultants to the group and set up a

resource pool for students to call for assistance with their difficult subjects. Make it clear that the group will terminate when all the members have improved their goals.

Be ready for a flood of resistance from members in the first few weeks of the group, but explain that any excessive absenteeism may require the group to meet for make-up sessions. The PIN approach requires patience and endurance, but usually results in a self-maintaining, highly cohesive group system.

*PIN FACT SHEET
*PIN stands for Peer Intervention Network

1. Who is in this group?
   This group is made up of kids who are bright, normal, not disturbed, and capable of succeeding in school. For various reasons, the members have not passed their subjects. Before this group ends, you will all know why and you will improve your grades.

2. The group's purpose and task:
   To assist each other in improving your school work.

3. The way we operate:
   a. Meet once or twice a week.
   b. Hear and react to progress reports.
   c. Explain what is blocking you and what you will do to unblock.
   d. Set up times of shadow contacts and teacher contacts.

4. Attendance is required at all sessions.

5. You must serve as a shadow to another group member. In your role as shadow, keep a record of all assignments and do everything legal and ethical to help your partner improve his or her work. Your partner cannot be your shadow, too. You must have a different shadow, not the one you supervise.

6. If, at the end of the marking period, you raise *all* your grades, you no longer need supervision and can drop your shadow. But, as an expert you remain in the group as someone else's shadow.

Permission to reprint Copyright © 1990, V. Alex Kehayan, *Self-Awareness Growth Experiences*, Jalmar Press, Rolling Hills Estates, CA.

7. If your shadow is not helping you, he or she must suffer the consequences, and can be fired, provided he or she can find another member who will accept his or her supervision (an even exchange).

8. You are in this together until school ends.

9. Each week you must report on how your plan is going and supply evidence of progress (grades on tests, and assignments). If things are not going well for any student, the group will meet to devise a new plan.

Good Luck!

Coordinator

Permission to reprint Copyright © 1990, V. Alex Kehayan, *Self-Awareness Growth Experiences*, Jalmar Press, Rolling Hills Estates, CA.

SELF — EVALUATION

Name: _____ Grade:_____

Who is your Shadow? _____

Subjects for which you
received Failure Notices: _____

_____

D Notices: _____

_____

What problems do you have with these subjects?

1. Homework _____

2. Understanding materials _____

3. Teacher _____

4. Class notes _____

5. Tests _____

Why are you failing?

_____

_____

_____

What has kept you from putting more effort into your studies?

_____

_____

_____

Permission to reprint Copyright © 1990, V. Alex Kehayan, *Self-Awareness Growth Experiences*, Jalmar Press, Rolling Hills Estates, CA.

PLAN OF ACTION

Date _____

Name _____   Phone # _____

Shadow's Name _____   Phone # _____

PLAN

Steps to be taken to improve your work:

1. _____

2. _____

3. _____

Steps to be taken by shadow to assist you:

1. _____

2. _____

3. _____

PROGRESS

Daily contacts with shadow

Date_____ Time _____ Place _____

Date_____ Time _____ Place _____

Date_____ Time _____ Place _____

Date_____ Time _____ Place _____

Dates of phone conversations: _____

_____

Dates of meetings and subject worked on:

Date _____ Subject _____

Date _____ Subject _____

Date _____ Subject _____

Date _____ Subject _____

Changes for next week: _____

_____

Permission to reprint Copyright © 1990, V. Alex Kehayan, *Self-Awareness Growth Experiences*, Jalmar Press, Rolling Hills Estates, CA.

7. Priorities Warm-Up

Ask the group to read the list of self-disclosure activities below and prioritize them from most to least appealing. Then, divide the group into fours, encouraging each member to initiate once icebreaker. Hold a discussion about the reasons for priority selections. Then, hold a re-run, this time encouraging each member to try out one of their lowest priorities in order to deal with their social anxiety. Discuss the feelings and rally support for the social risk takers.

Risky Warm-Ups

Talk about the best book you've ever read.

Imitate the clucking of a chicken.

Talk about three of your best qualities.

Do a silent pantomime of your entire morning wake-up routine.

Tell a joke.

Talk about a frustrating experience.

Act out, non-verbally, what it feels like to be here now.

Permission to reprint Copyright © 1990, V. Alex Kehayan, *Self-Awareness Growth Experiences*, Jalmar Press, Rolling Hills Estates, CA.

Resource Activities*	Reference Codes	Grade Levels
1. Play Ball	HV, pp. 68-71	7-12
2. Trust Walk	BVC, p. 79	7-12
3. Broken Squares	HB I, pp. 25-29	7-12
4. Toothpicks	HB IV, pp. 99-102	7-12
5. Learning Teams	DHP, pp. 73-74	7-12
6. What Do You Know? What Do You Want to Know?	DHP, pp. 75-77	7-12
7. Blackboard Role Play	RP, pp. 49-53	7-8
8. Social Studies: Minority Groups or Poverty	CVSM, pp. 55-59	7-8
9. Peer Teaching-Learning Center	DHP II, pp. 77-78	7-12
10. Add a Movement, Sound, or Shape	GFF, pp. 132-135	7-12
11. Working with Obstacles	GFF, pp. 141-142	7-12
12. Follow the Leader (II)	GFF, pp. 155-156	7-12
13. Teacher Role Checklist for Cooperative Instruction	LTA, pp. 123-124	7-12
14. Sharing and Supporting Goals	DHR, pp. 87-89	10-12

*See Appendix B.

OBJECTIVE 5

TO STRENGTHEN PEER RELATIONSHIPS

STRATEGIES

1. Forced Cooperation

    As a way of reducing conflict between two students who have shown antagonism toward each other, assign the adversaries to a joint task which they must complete cooperatively within a strict time limit. A single grade is issued to both students when the task is completed. This procedure will encourage the antagonists to find methods of working out the conflicts while engaged in a collaborative effort.

2. Popularity Opinion Poll[16]

    To identify group members' attributes which improve peer relationships, ask students to close their eyes and imagine someone who they know to be popular. Then request students to list on paper the qualities, behaviors, and features which they admire. No names are to be used. Use the lists to develop a collective inventory of characteristics admired by the group.

    Repeat this exercise about every two months to determine the changes in popularity factors. As the level of trust increases ask members to name peers whom they view as popular.

[16]This strategy was developed by Marcia Wyrtzen, staff therapist, Center for Creative Living, Allendale, N.J., and Linda Max De Sheplo. Adapted by permission of the authors.

3. Observation Technique

    When engaging the student in any group exercise, use the fishbowl technique. Ask student observers to surround the working groups and respond to the questions on the following Guideline sheet.

PROCESS OBSERVATION GUIDELINES[17]

   I. Event _____

  II. Object _____

 III. Participation
      A. Who talked the most?
      B. Did all have opportunities to participate?
      C. Were some excluded?
      D. Was an effort made to draw people out?
      E. Did a few dominate?
      F. Did the non-talkers appear to be listening?

  IV. Communication
      A. Did people feel free to talk?
      B. Was there any interrupting or cutting people off?
      C. Did people listen to others?
      D. Was there clarification of points made?
      E. Was there any attempt to hold together various ideas?
      F. Did people openly confront one another and give honest feedback?

   V. Suggestions
      A. Can you think of any ways to improve the quality of participation?
      B. Can you suggest ways to improve the communication?

[17]These Guidelines were suggested by Michael Villano, chairman, Social Studies Department, Fort Lee High School, Fort Lee, N.J. Adapted by permission of the author.

After the exercise, have the observers give feedback to the participants and make suggestions for improvement.

4. The Come-On Game[18]

To sensitize students to the adverse effects of sexist type behavior, initiate a role reversal simulation. Ask all girls in the group to form a circle with each member facing outward. Explain that since the boys are so well practiced in looking over the girls, this experience gives the girls an opportunity to take on male roles.

[18]This strategy was developed by Michael Villano, chairman, Social Studies Department, Fort Lee High School, Fort Lee, N.J. Adapted by permission of the author.

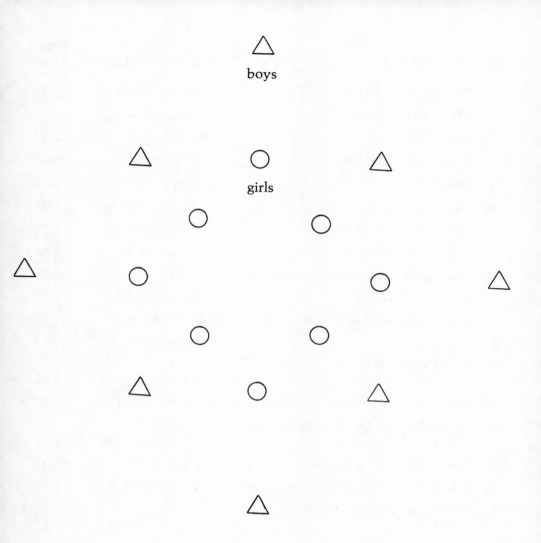

boys

girls

Instruct the boys to parade around the circle while the girls stalk them, give them "the eye," and make sly comments. The comments may be provocative but not profane. No body contact is allowed.

After five minutes of milling around, ask each girl to select a boy and accompany him to a corner of the room. Each couple is then given five minutes to role play a first meeting situation.

Hold a discussion to elicit reactions to the experience. Emphasize the feelings and conflicts inherent in being passed up, chosen, and getting acquainted.

Conclude with suggestions on how to make male/female relationships more comfortable and empathetic.

Resource Activities*	Reference Codes	Grade Levels
1. Exploring Sex Roles	DHP, pp. 31-32	9-12
2. The Perfect Square	DHP II, pp. 44-45	7-12
3. Out of Bounds	DHP II, p. 47	7-12
4. Handcuffed Together	DHP II, p. 61	7-12
5. Boxed-In	BVC, pp. 124-126	7-12
6. Authority Figure	BVC, pp. 132-134	7-12
7. Facing Human Sexuality	BVC, pp. 147-151	9-12
8. I Can Make Contact	LHT, pp. 88-89	7-12
9. Frustrating Games (once per month)	LHT, pp. 102-103	7-9
10. Boys and Girls	LHT, p. 100	7-12
11. Killer Statements and Gestures	100, pp. 67-68	7-12
12. Quickies	100, pp. 85-87	7-12
13. Males Versus Females Facts Versus Myths	UYO, p. 1	9-12
14. Assessing Your Interpersonal Stress	UYO, pp. 69-71	9-12
15. What Qualities Do You Desire in a Mate?	UYO, pp. 141-142	9-12
16. Your Kind of People	AE, pp. 42-43	10-12
17. Add a Movement, Sound, or Shape	GFF, pp. 134-135	7-12
18. Moving in Response to Group Directions	GFF, pp. 139-141	7-12
19. Solving Human Relations Problems in the Personalized Classroom	PE, pp. 60-64	7-12
20. Male/Female Roles	DAE, pp. 97-102	10-12
21. Learning to Love	DAE, p. 305	9-12
22. Sexual Codes	DAE, pp. 313-315	7-12
23. Adjectives	ICE, pp. 69-70	7-12

*See Appendix B.

OBJECTIVE 6

TO SUSTAIN FRIENDSHIPS WITH PEERS

STRATEGIES

1. Teaching Compromises

To encourage negotiation and compromise as ways to sustain relationships with others, ask the students to try this exercise.

Direct the students to write down situations where different opinions or needs caused conflicts in relationships with friends, teachers, parents or others. Some examples might include:

1. Shopping with a friend who wants to go to different stores than you do.
2. Clash of interests in preferences for an activity.
3. A conflict with parent regarding clothing, i.e., you see four pants you like, but can only buy three.
4. Friend wants to go to different film than you do.

Ask the group to break up in pairs and role play how to resolve a given conflict by negotiating and compromising. Students write down the solution and report to the group on how it was reached. Discuss the values and techniques of compromise on a broader scale.

2. The Complainer[19]

Ask the group to read and develop their responses to the following passage and imagine how they might react to the situation.

The Complainer
You have a close friend who always seems to go through rough times. You have known him since kindergarten. You belong to the same church and share many other common interests and activities. Your friend recently broke up with his

[19]This strategy was developed by Dr. Peter Wolf, psychologist, private practice, New York, New York. Adapted by permission of the author.

girlfriend and all he does is talk about how miserable he feels. You are bored and tired of listening to him. You are thinking of ditching the friendship, but you would feel badly if you stopped trying to support him.

After about fifteen minutes hold a discussion to elicit the group's reactions. Emphasize the following questions:

1. How should this person decide whether or not to save the friendship?
2. What are some of the ingredients of a good friendship?
3. Can a friendship weather a storm such as this?
4. What would you do if this person was your friend?

3. The Book of Friends[20]

Ask the group to create experience books about their friends. Gather as many cameras as possible and instruct the students to photograph two friends, include them in Books of Friends, and write a character sketch about each one. The sketches should respond to the following questions:

1. How did you meet?
2. What do you like about your friends?
3. What don't you like?
4. How long would you like to be friends?
5. How long do you think you will be friends?
6. How can you help the friendship to continue?

Spend two or three periods discussing the value of sustaining friendships. Be sensitive not to embarrass new group members or those students who have not developed friendships. Make this a voluntary experience.

It may be worthwhile to explain this idea to various camera manufacturers and ask them to donate cameras for this project.

[20]This strategy was developed by James Warnke, M.S.W. psychotherapist, Teaneck, N.J. Used by permission of the author.

Resource Activities*	Reference Codes	Grade Levels
1. Questions to Get to Know Someone Better	DHP, pp. 15-16	7-12
2. Commonalities	DHP, p. 16	7-12
3. Want Ad	BVC, pp. 98-99	7-12
4. Peer Perceptions	HB III, pp. 41-45	7-12
5. Your Kind of People	AE, pp. 41-43	10-12
6. Knowing Your Peers	AE, pp. 44-45	10-12
7. Teacher Role Checklist for Cooperative Instruction	LTA, pp. 123-124	7-12

*See Appendix B.

OBJECTIVE 7

TO RESPOND POSITIVELY TO TEACHERS AND OTHER AUTHORITY FIGURES

STRATEGIES

1. Supportive Parent Conferences

   Initiate parent-teacher-child conferences to exchange positive feedback regarding school issues. Ask parents to identify what they see as their child's major strengths and potentials. Help the parents to develop a list of experiences which are enjoyable to both parents and child.

   As a follow-up, encourage the parents and child to share one positive experience each week. Examples of such experiences include: a weekend outing, a shopping spree, and a hike through the woods.

2. Use of Positive Feedback

   Employ various approaches to strengthen your relationships with students. Acknowledge positive behaviors, such as problem-solving, topic-oriented discussions, sustained attention, and listening to others.

   Remember to focus on the students who show positive behavior by smiling, winking, moving to close proximity, shaking hands, and maintaining eye contact.

3. Reflections of a Veteran Teacher[21]

   Distribute copies of the passage below to the group and ask a member to read the contents aloud. Then initiate a discussion to sensitize the students to this teacher's perspective.

---

[21]This strategy was developed by Michael Villano, chairman, Social Studies Department, Fort Lee High School, Fort Lee, N.J., and this author collaboratively. Adapted by permission from the authors.

The mercenary hardly ever attended my class, and when he did, he rarely spoke. The gambler was the editor of the school newspaper. The priest was the captain of the football team. The bank robber always made people laugh with his corny jokes. The junkie just sat in class with a vacant stare.

The mercenary was killed in Angola several years ago. The gambler is now on welfare. The priest was stabbed to death at a counseling home for runaways. The bank robber is in jail. The junkie has not been heard from in five years and his family has disowned him.

All these students sat in front of me at one time or another while I taught them the parts of speech and tested their vocabulary knowledge. I wonder how I might have helped them to become better human beings.

Questions for Discussion

1. If you were this teacher's personal adviser, what kind of advice might you give?
2. Do you think this teacher had a negative effect on these students?
3. What, if anything, could this teacher have done to help these students?
4. How do you think this teacher feels?

4. Visual Squash

Ask group members to use the following visualization techniques to prevent hostile outbursts at authority figures who are hard to deal with.

Visualize the people who trigger your anger reactions in a new, compromising, or outrageous setting. Use visualization to change them into cartoon-like characters, with pink mustaches and purple ears. Make them black and white instead of in color. Or put them in the distance by imagining them far away, or out of focus.

Resource Activities*	Reference Codes	Grade Levels
1. Letters to Teachers	HV, p. 97	7-12
2. Authority Figure	BVC, pp. 132-134	7-12
3. My Most Unforgetable Teacher	AE, pp. 55-56	7-12
4. Establishing Identity (I)	GFF, pp. 235-236	7-12
5. Solving Human Relations Problems in the Personalized Classroom	PE, pp. 60-64	7-12
6. Teacher Feedback	100, pp. 78-79	7-8
7. Caterpillar Race	ICE, pp. 17-18	7-12

* See Appendix B.

GOAL IV

To Develop Problem-Solving and Decision-Making Skills

Problem-solving and decision-making are joined in this section because of their inherent relationship to each other. The solutions to life's dilemmas frequently entail some type of choice or decision-making process.

SAGE: SELF-AWARENESS GROWTH EXPERIENCES focuses on the basic skills which help students to address their developmental conflicts. The six objectives are presented in a hierarchical sequence which should be followed by the group leader. Standardized test profiles in students' permanent records should provide the necessary data to choose the appropriate entry objectives.

In this section is an array of techniques designed to marshal the students' natural creativity and inventiveness in solving problems and making intelligent decisions. The materials and approaches focus on sequences of events, data collection methods, priorities, testing assumptions, and learning about consequential outcomes of behavior.

Many of the objectives and strategies in this section employ the analysis, synthesis, and evaluation skills found at the three highest levels of Bloom's (1956) Taxonomy. These skills are helpful in identifying problems, clarifying goals, and predicting potential outcomes of decisions.

In this section are a number of situations which focus on conflicts faced by adolescents. These include confrontations with friends and authority figures; conflicts involving political, moral, and social issues; and dilemmas revolving around individual identity.

The major emphasis is on the exploration of students' own values, needs, and aspirations as they apply to the many decisions they face in their lives. The strategies employ brainstorming, role playing, and simulation approaches. They also lend themselves to the fishbowl observation technique.

It is important to encourage students to share their own decisions with the group and to pass on their own methods of making decisions. Feel free to draw on the material in other sections (To Develop Creativity and To Develop Ethical Standards) for techniques applicable to the issues in this section.

OBJECTIVE 1

TO RECOGNIZE WHEN A CONFLICT SITUATION EXISTS IN STORIES, HYPOTHETICAL CASES, OR ROLE-PLAYING ACTIVITIES

STRATEGIES

1. To Speak or Not to Speak[22]

   To heighten students' awareness of personal conflicts, ask them to imagine themselves in a history class. Pose the dilemma of what to do when you think you know the answer but are ambivalent about whether or not to raise your hand or remain silent. Ask students to rehearse their unspoken dialogues.

   Follow up with a discussion inquiring about the cause of their conflict, such as putting oneself on the line, risking embarrassment, or receiving criticism from others. These issues should be discussed as major precipitators of conflicts.

2. On the Spot[23]

   Distribute Problem Sheets to students. Ask them to read the problem and write down their interpretation of the conflict. Instruct them to list as many facets of the problem as possible.

   [22]This strategy was developed by Michael Villano, chairman, Social Studies Department, Fort Lee High School, Fort Lee, N.J. Adapted by permission of the author.

   [23]This strategy was developed by Dr. Peter Wolf, psychologist, private practice, New York, New York. Adapted by permission of the author.

Problem Sheet

On the Spot

You are an adult and your father has just passed away, leaving your mother a widow. You never really got along with your mother and the relationship has always been a source of discomfort. Your mother, feeling helpless and distressed, has asked if she could live with you for a while until she recovers from the loss of your father.

After about fifteen minutes, lead a discussion to identify the factors in this situation that might cause personal conflicts. Include the following questions:

1. Have you ever known someone who lost a parent?

2. How did they react?

3. If you were facing this situation, what would be your concerns?

4. What would be the most difficult part of the problem to face?

5. What might be the results of your decision?

3. The Wake-Up Conflict[24]

To heighten the awareness of everyday conflicts, ask students to imagine themselves in bed on a Monday morning. Proceed with the following passage:

The alarm rings and you are faced with the decision: If you get up immediately, you can have a nice shower, leisurely breakfast, and arrive at school on time. But, you are tired and the other part of you says, "I don't really need a shower. I just had one yesterday. If I skip it, I can sleep for ten more minutes."

Ask the students to rehearse their personal unspoken debates. Elicit reactions that express the conflicting issues.

[24]This strategy was developed by Michael Villano, chairman, Social Studies Department, Fort Lee High School, Fort Lee, N.J. Used by permission of the author.

Resource Activities*	Reference Codes	Grade Levels
1. Literature	CVSM, pp. 44-47	9-12
2. Immediate Physical Setting Role Play	NM, pp. 30-31	9-12
3. Prescription for the Future	D (LG), p. 12 D, pp. 5-6	9-12
4. To Decide or Hang Loose	D (LG), pp. 12-14 D, pp. 7-8	9-12
5. The Story of Missed Decisions	D (LG), p. 14 D, pp. 9-10	9-12
6. Decisions — An Open-Chair Role Play	RP, pp. 13-46	7-12

*See Appendix B.

OBJECTIVE 2

TO USE ADDITIONAL INFORMATION IN MAKING DECISIONS AND SOLVING PROBLEMS

STRATEGIES

1. Anonymous Advisors (A.A.)[25]

    This exercise is intended to promote student cooperation in seeking alternative solutions. Because of the controversial nature of some adolescent dilemmas, this strategy restricts its material to academic problems.

    Preparation:

    1. Cover one shoe box with red construction paper and label it "Problems."

    2. Cover another shoe box with green construction paper and label it "Alternatives."

    3. Print fifty Information Sheets using the following format:

INFORMATION SHEET (side 1)	INFORMATION SHEET (side 2)
Date Submitted: Code Name: Please provide alternative solutions to the following academic problem:	Date Submitted: Here are some alternative solutions to your academic problem: 1. 2. 3. 4. 5. Remember *only you* can make the final decision on how to resolve your problem.

    4. Place shoeboxes and Information Sheets on a table or desk in a corner of the room.

    5. Solicit five student volunteers who meet the following criteria:

        a. Interested in helping others
        b. Demonstrate good brainstorming and problem-solving techniques
        c. Available for after-school meetings

    6. Enlist the aid of a guidance counselor or other colleague who may assist you in supervising this program.

---

[25]This strategy was developed by Carolyn Kehayan, special education teacher, Fort Lee Public Schools, Fort Lee, N.J. Used by permission of the author.

Present to group as follows:

We are going to try working together to provide an anonymous advisory service. The service will offer alternative solutions to any student's academic problems, for example, studying for tests, writing reports, preparing speeches, homework strategies, and improving grades. Our five volunteers (name students) will be the student advisors for this month. We will rotate advisors every month on a voluntary basis. A teacher will serve as an ongoing consultant and supervisor for the advisor group.

If you would like to seek alternative solutions to an academic dilemma, you can fill out one of the Information Sheets. To insure anonymity, please write a code name on the top of the sheet. Then describe the academic difficulty in the space provided and place the Information Sheet in the red Problem Box.

Every two days, student advisors will meet after school to brainstorm at least two alternative solutions to the submitted problems. Advisors, with the assistance of one teacher, will write their suggestions on the reverse side of the Information Sheet and will place them in the green Alternatives Box.

After a two-day period, you may retrieve your Information Sheet from the green box. Your problem and the alternative solutions will remain anonymous. Please keep in mind that the primary task of the advisory service is to provide you with more than one possible alternative to your problem. However, it is your responsibility to determine if any of the suggested alternatives are useful and to implement the strategy you decide is best.

Note: The advisory service may want to write down the alternatives they have suggested and place them in an ongoing file according to academic problem categories. This file then becomes a bank of suggestions to which the class can refer.

2. Group Problem Analysis[26]

Call the group together to pose and solve manageable problems that are interrupting the educational task at hand. Have each student bring a list of his or her pressing problems that have the potential to be resolved. Encourage verbal exchange of each member's perceived problem, and enlist the support of the class to decide on which problem to focus.

Once a decision is reached, ask each student to list the major forces which block the problem from being solved. Also, ask students to list the resources that might help to solve the problem. Call the group together to reach a consensus on the major forces. Each member then lists ways that the resources of the group can be marshaled to solve a particular problem.

Also, ask each student to list ways to overcome the blocking forces. Call together the group to discuss the negative forces and the positive resources, and to establish a plan to resolve the problem.

After some action is taken, call short meetings to monitor the problem-solving plan as it progresses.

Example
Problem: Lateness to first period class
Solution Goal: To improve punctuality

Resources	*Blocking Forces*
1. Alarm clocks	1. Late nights
2. The punctual students	2. Poor eating habits
3.	3. Only one bathroom in the house
4.	4.
5.	5.

Plan:
1. Enlist the aid of more prompt students to phone the late students each morning, or team up with them in some way.
2. Go to bed ten minutes earlier each week.
3.
4.
5.

---

[26]This strategy is a modified form of the Force-Field Analysis, a method developed by Kurt Lewin and cited in "Force Field Analysis" by Sallie E. Tancil in NEA Journal. Vol. 57, No. 3 (March 1968), pp. 23-27. Adapted by permission of publisher.

3. The Missing Watch[27]

   To emphasize information gathering skills, ask students to imagine themselves in this situation:

   > You are lying in bed one night and you suddenly realize that your watch is not on the night table where you usually place it. You search the house, but to no avail. As you mentally scan the events of the day, you remember putting on the watch in the morning and having it during your first three classes. You also remember using someone else's locker during gym class. You do not remember whether you had it on after gym, but you do remember your other activities which include swimming, doing homework at your friend's house and eating dinner at home. You are just not sure when or where the watch disappeared.

   After they have read about the situation, ask students to break into small groups and write down their responses to the following questions:

   1. What questions would you need to ask to guide you in your search?
   2. Which questions would help you to narrow down the possibilities?
   3. Which questions might be unproductive?

   Encourage brainstorming as an aid to the process. After about fifteen minutes, bring the group together, share the responses, and ask the students to develop a collective list of the most productive questions.

   [27]This strategy was developed by Dr. Peter Wolf, psychologist, private practice, New York, New York. Used by permission of the author.

Resource Activities*	Reference Codes	Grade Levels
1. Fall-Out Shelter Problem	VC, pp. 281-287	7-12
2. Hospital's Bonanza	CGG, p. 26	7-12
3. Guidelines for Goal Setting	100, pp. 188-189	9-12
4. Decisions — Open-Chair Brainstorm	HV, pp. 171-175	9-12
5. Identifying Alternatives	D (LG), p. 22 D, p. 21	9-12
6. Alternatives and Related Information	D (LG), p. 24 D, p. 25	9-12

OBJECTIVE 3

TO EXPRESS ALTERNATE SOLUTIONS TO CONFLICT SITUATIONS

STRATEGIES

1. Cause and Effect Exercise

    When reading stories and history lessons, assign students the task of brainstorming and recording possible causes for the historical events and alternative endings to the stories. Ask the students to describe what they perceive to be the causes of conflicts, the resulting emotions that emerge from them, and how the characters affect each other.

2. Captionless Comics[28]

    Collect several comic strips depicting unresolved situations and conflicts between characters. Make copies of each comic strip, blocking out all captions on the duplicate sheets. Divide the class into pairs and distribute the original and captionless copies to each dyad. Have students read and analyze each dilemma presented in the original comic. Their task is to resolve or improve the situation presented by rewriting the captions on the duplicate sheet.

    When the activity is completed, display original and student-modified comics on the bulletin board, in the school newspaper, or in booklet form. Follow-up with a discussion on how dialogue can be improved to achieve more effective communication.

    Note: You may want to use the following variations of this exercise:

    1. Have students delete, change, or rearrange comic strip pictures in addition to modifying captions.
    2. Have talented art students draw the pictures as well as write the captions for the comic strips.

---

[28]This strategy was developed by Carolyn Kehayan, special education teacher, Fort Lee Public Schools, Fort Lee, N.J. Used by permission of the author.

3. Draw original comics illustrating conflict issues experienced by your group or class. Have students rewrite captions to show better alternatives. Discuss how these alternatives could be implemented within the classroom setting.

3. Friends or Lovers[29]

Set the stage for this event by asking students to recall a situation in which they were affected by a rumor about someone very close to them. Then spend a session engaging the group in an alternative-seeking activity. Distribute copies of the following passage to the group and allow ten minutes for students to reflect and generate alternative reactions.

Friends or Lovers

Roger and Ginny have been seeing each other for a year. They are very serious. Roger's best friend, John, has just broken up with his girlfriend, Lauren, and is feeling very lonely and depressed. Roger and John have been best friends for five years. They are on the track team together and their parents are also close friends.

One day Roger is in the locker room and notices people staring at him knowingly. Later that day he overhears one of the kids in school telling another that Ginny and John were seen together three times in one day, once at the local 7-Eleven, again at Burger King, and later walking down the street. Roger looks puzzled and walks away from the conversation.

After students have reflected for ten minutes, lead a brainstorming activity to generate possible strategies that Roger might use in dealing with this situation.

[29]This strategy was developed by Dr. Peter Wolf, psychologist, private practice, New York, New York. Adapted by permission of the author.

4. Visual Rehearsal

Ask students to use rehearsal techniques to run through the upcoming challenge by trying out the way in which they would to apply the solution.

Resource Activities*	Reference Codes	Grade Levels
1. Marijuana Story	HV, pp. 180-183	7-12
2. Value Decisions	NM, pp. 132-133	9-12
3. Alligator River Episode	NM, pp. 140-145	7-12
4. What Did They Solve?	AB, pp. 31-33	7-8
5. Last Period Class	AB, pp. 36-37	7-12
6. What Are Some Alternatives?	AB, pp. 38-40	7-8
7. Identifying Alternatives	D (LG), p. 22 D, p.21	9-12
8. Do You Know All the Alternatives?	D (LG), pp. 22-24	9-12
9. Options — A Decision-Making Game	D (LG), p. 22-24 D (LG), p. 22	9-12
10. Graduation Alternatives	D (LG), p. 22 D, p.24	9-12
11. Options Paper	DHP II, pp. 72-74	9-12
12. Diamonds and Rubies	CGG, p. 26-27	7-12
13. Hospital's Bonanza	CGG, p. 48	9-12
14. The Shipwrecked Sailor	CGG, pp. 49-50	9-12
15. Lost on the Moon — A Group Consensus Task	UYO, pp. 104-105	7-12
16. Consensus	TLC, p. 54	7-12

*See Appendix B.

OBJECTIVE 4

TO EXPRESS PREFERENCES IN PERSONAL CHOICES AND GOALS

STRATEGIES

1. Weekly Reaction Sheets

   To assist group members in developing personal goals and taking responsibility for self-improvement, ask each student to fill out a Weekly Reaction Sheet. The form monitors personal development; use of time, energy and resources; and clarifies the student's sense of direction. Monitor and discuss at regular intervals to note changes. A model group reaction sheet follows.

Weekly Reaction Sheet

Name: _____ Date: _____

1. What was the high point of the week?

    _____

    _____

    _____

2. Whom did you get to know better this week?

    _____

    _____

    _____

3. What was the major thing you learned about yourself this week?

    _____

    _____

    _____

4. Did you institute any major changes in your life this week?

    _____

    _____

    _____

5. How could this week have been better?

    _____

    _____

Permission to reprint Copyright © 1990, V. Alex Kehayan, *Self-Awareness Growth Experiences*, Jalmar Press, Rolling Hills Estates, CA.

6. What did you procrastinate about this week?

_____

_____

_____

7. Identify three decisions or choices you made this week. What were the results of these choices?

_____

_____

_____

_____

8. Did you make any plans this week for some future event?

_____

_____

_____

9. What unfinished personal business do you have left from this last week? How long have you been carrying it? How long do you plan to carry it?

_____

_____

_____

_____

Permission to reprint Copyright © 1990, V. Alex Kehayan, *Self-Awareness Growth Experiences*, Jalmar Press, Rolling Hills Estates, CA.

2. Reaching Agreement

Ask the group to reach a unanimous agreement on a list of myths and assumptions which they generate. Invite each member to jot down one favorite life assumption which he or she believes to be true. Then compile a list, distribute to the group, and ask members to reach total acceptance or total rejection of each assumption.

Some of the statements might include:
1. All red-haired people have hot tempers.
2. All good things come with effort.
3. All people with foreign accents are stupid.
4. Everything always turns out for the best.
5. People do things for lack of anything better to do.

After the group has attempted to reach consensus on some of the statements, lead a general discussion on how difficult it was to reach a unanimous decision, what factors enhanced or blocked the process; and what feelings arose out of the experience.

3. The Stereo Dilemma

Ask students to imagine themselves faced with the prospect of selecting and buying a stereo system. Each student is to write a list of factors and information necessary to make such a decision. Then initiate a discussion identifying the unique ways in which decisions depend on individual preferences and personal priorities.

Resource Activities*	Reference Codes	Grade Levels
1. Pie of Life	VC, pp. 228-231	7-12
2. Fall-Out Shelter Problem	VC, pp. 281-286	7-12
3. A Problem for NASA	AB, pp. 6-7	7-12
4. Guidelines for Goal Setting	100, pp. 188-189	9-12
5. Hopes Whip	HV, p. 92	9-12
6. What I Want to Be Like	NM, p. 88	9-12
7. History — The Civil War	CVSM, pp. 52-54	7-12
8. Individual Goal Setting	ICE, pp. 373-376	7-12
9. Caro	TLC, p. 56	7-12

*See Appendix B.

OBJECTIVE 5

TO EXPLAIN REASONS FOR SELECTING ALTERNATIVES

STRATEGIES

1. Alternative Reactions

To discriminate between alternative ways of behaving, make a ditto master with pictures and phrases to provide situations and choices of behavior students may follow. Run off copies and have students circle one choice and then rationalize it.

Example 1: Peter has just struck out three times in an informal baseball game with some friends. He wears a frown and is seated on the grass some distance from the other players. Pretending you are his teammate, what can you do? (a) You could say, "Hello"; (b) You could talk to him; (c) You could hit him; (d) You could make fun of him; (e) You could ask, "Can I help you?"; (f) You could walk with him; (g) You could say, "Why did you come here? Go away!"

Example 2: Jeff has a little brother, Andy. Sometimes Andy makes Jeff angry. Andy gets into Jeff's things. What can Jeff do? (a) Jeff can try to keep things where Andy cannot get them; (b) Jeff can hit Andy; (c) Jeff can talk to his mother; (d) Jeff can make Andy cry; (e) Jeff can play with Andy now and then; (f) Jeff can think, "Oh, well, Andy is little; he does not always know what to do and what not to do."

Initiate general discussions revolving around how the people in these situations might benefit or suffer from various ways of reacting to others.

2. On the Other Hand[30]

This exercise enables students to review critically popular viewpoints on major issues. Present one of the Issue Statements below and ask group members to use brainstorming to develop three alternative viewpoints.

Issue Statements

1. In order to deter all violent crimes, capital punishment should be instituted throughout the nation.

2. It is the responsibility of the United States to provide aid to homeless refugees.

3. As the population increases, many wildlife preserves will have to be utilized for building homes and/or obtaining food and fuel resources.

4. Busing is the best means to attain social and academic equality among all racial groups.

5. Increased taxes are needed to provide more services for the elderly poor.

6. Despite the F.D.A. ban on various experimental cancer drugs, decisions regarding use should be left to the individual patient and his or her family.

7. All nuclear reactor plants should shut down until more in-depth safety investigations are undertaken.

8. The draft is the best method of achieving a strong, well-balanced army.

9. In order to insure national security and an optimal defense system, the type and quantity of U.S. armaments should not be made public.

For example, the alternative viewpoints for Issue 1 might include:

1A. In order to deter all violent crimes, more life prison sentences should be issued to serious offenders.

2A. In order to deter all violent crimes, stricter gun control laws are required.

3A. In order to deter all violent crimes, more and better social programs should be instituted.

---

[30]This strategy was developed by Carolyn Kehayan, special education teacher, Fort Lee Public Schools, Fort Lee, N.J. Used by permission of the author.

Divide the students into the three groups and assign each group one of these viewpoints. Members of each group do not necessarily have to believe in the alternative they are assigned. Allow groups fifteen minutes to generate and list three reasons for supporting the assigned viewpoint. For example, three reasons for supporting Alternative 1A might include:

1. Potential offenders will be too afraid to commit crimes because they will know a serious offense will cost them more than a few years in prison.

2. There will be less acts of violence because the serious offenders will be locked up for life and will not have the opportunity to repeat their crimes.

3. Life imprisonment is more of a deterrent than capital punishment because the criminal knows his or her term of suffering will endure longer than if he or she were put to death.

Ask a spokesperson for each group to share their supporting data with the entire membership. Initiate a short debate during which the three groups challenge each other's assigned viewpoints and supporting statements. Conclude by taking a poll of actual personal preferences to each of the alternatives discussed.

Follow this procedure for each of the Issue Statements.

3. Problem-Solving Group

To provide practice in generating reasons for choosing alternative solutions, set up problem-solving networks by assigning students to groups of four. Members assume roles of "client," "counselor," and two "observers." The person in the role of client poses a current, relevant, and reality-oriented dilemma which must be addressed by the counselor. Stress the importance of honesty, concern, and empathy as appropriate conditions. At the end of a twenty-minute session, each observer reports the options, decisions, their rationales, and the outcomes of the exercise. It is good idea to have students rotate roles in subsequent sessions.

Resource Activities*	Reference Codes	Grade Levels
1. Cash Register: Group Decision Making	HB V, pp. 10-12	9-12
2. Goal Dyads	HV, p. 93	7-12
3. Decisions — Open-Chair Brainstorm	HV, pp. 171-175	9-12
4. Marijuana Story	HV, pp. 180-183	7-12
5. Acceptable and Unacceptable Alternatives	D (LG), p. 25 D, p. 26	9-12
6. Solving the Joe Doodlebug Problem	UYO, p. 20	7-12
7. Time Capsule	PE, pp. 242-243	7-12
8. Issue-Centered Writing	SCL, pp. 145-153	7-12

*See Appendix B.

OBJECTIVE 6

TO EVALUATE CRITICALLY THE RISKS AND CONSEQUENCES OF MAKING A DECISION

STRATEGIES

1. <u>First Strike Scenario</u>

   Describe some every-day situations which call for immediate decisions. Such decisions might be necessary to avoid accidents, defend oneself, or deal with peer pressure. Then, ask the group to imagine themselves facing the following dilemma:

   > You are the President of the United States. One morning at three o'clock, you receive a call from the Secretary of Defense. He informs you that our Early Warning System has flashed a signal that the Soviets have launched several ICBM's which are moving toward our country and will arrive in approximately thirty minutes. The reports suggest that they are targeted toward our missile sites. The Secretary informs you that if you authorize a counter attack, our missiles could destroy a good portion of the Soviet's remaining missiles. But, millions of Soviet civilians could perish as a result. The other option is to use our defensive missiles to destroy the oncoming Soviet missiles. In either case, the death toll will be astronomical.

   Ask the students to list the potential consequences of both a decision to counterattack and a decision to use our defensive anti-aircraft system. After students have identified the potential implications of each action, hold a discussion to reach a consensus on how the President should react.

2. The Governor's Dilemma

Ask the group to imagine themselves faced with the following situation:

> You are the Governor of California and have been asked to issue a stay of execution for a criminal on death row. You have been told that, although the jury has convicted the criminal of first degree murder, the defense claims to be awaiting important testimony which could clear the suspect of the charge. The criminal has a long record of serious violent crimes.

Ask each student to write down the risks and consequences involved in the Governor's dilemma. Discuss with the students their views of the situation and what factors they consider most important in the decision-making process. See if a consensus can be reached.

3. The Concerned Teacher[31]

Distribute copies of the following story to the group and initiate a brainstorming activity to generate alternative ways the teacher might respond.

> Mrs. Rogers, a high school teacher, is well liked by her students because she relates honestly and treats them with great respect.
>
> John is an outstanding student in Mrs. Rogers' class. He often confides in her.
>
> One day after class he speaks to her about some problems he has with his parents. He tells her that he plans to run away from home the following day. He assures Mrs. Rogers that he will be safe and will phone her after he has found a place to stay.

Ask the group to discuss some optional ways for Mrs. Rogers to respond to the situation:

1. Phone John's parents immediately and tell them what he intends to do.

2. Ask the guidance counselor to persuade John to work things out with his parents.

3. Explain the situation to John's friends and ask them to convince him to change his mind.

4. Wait until John phones her. Then encourage him to get in touch with his parents.

Encourage the group to brainstorm other optional ways for Mrs. Rogers to deal with this problem. Ask them to describe the potential risks and consequences of each reaction.

[31]This strategy was developed by Carolyn Kehayan, special education teacher, Fort Lee Public Schools, Fort Lee, N.J. Used by permission of the author.

4. The Word is No: Consequences of Chemical Dependency

To assist students in identifying the consequences of pursuing a chemically dependent lifestyle, read "The Word is No" drug and alcohol party scenario and then ask them to respond. After each member has had an opportunity to list some of the potential consequences of chemical use and abuse, lead a discussion which identifies and expands some of the potential consequences that could occur. They should include at least two of the following possibilities:

1. Somebody overdoses and has to be taken to the emergency ward of the local hospital.

2. You join in the fun and get so involved that you forget about your parents and are late to meet them when they come to pick you up.

3. The police search for you and find you, at your parents' request. When they finally catch up to you, they also bust your friends for substance and alcohol abuse. You all go to the police station.

4. Your parents have to pay a lot of money to get you out of the police station. They are very angry with you and yell at you when you get home.

5. You have to go to court for substance abuse by minors.

You are at a local amusement park with a bunch of friends and their older brothers and sisters. You have enjoyed many of the rides, including the roller coaster, the haunted house, the bumper cars, and several of the more exciting attractions.

You have just spent some time on playing games and winning prizes, laughing, and trading stories with your friends. As you are walking with a group of your friends, one of your closest friend's sisters arrives on the scene. A good-looking cheerleader, she's popular and well-liked by many people in high school. You feel really excited that she has stopped to talk with you. She tells your group about a really great party that's about to begin in an out-of-the way place nearby. She invites you all to join her and some of the older kids decide to share in the fun.

You are not sure what to do. All of a sudden, you notice a lot of your friends jump to the occasion and so you go with the group. You end up under the boardwalk where you see a few older teenagers, most of whom are couples, breaking out six-packs of beer and passing around marijuana cigarettes to each other.

Suddenly you remember that your parents will be waiting for you at the entrance to the park in about half an hour. As you're thinking of this, you find a full beer can thrust in your hands.

This is closely followed by a marijuana joint which is being passed around the group. You hear instructions from your friends about how to inhale. You hear coughing from other members of the group. Then you hear lots of laughing and see silly behavior.

Now pretend you can make a giant movie screen in your head. Imagine you are there now. Stop the action and freeze the scene on your personal screen with all the sights and sounds and colors. Think of some of the negative results that could occur if your were to join in the fun and get involved in this drug and alcohol party. Write some of them down on the lines below.

Permission to reprint Copyright © 1990, V. Alex Kehayan, *Self-Awareness Growth Experiences*, Jalmar Press, Rolling Hills Estates, CA.

Resource Activities*	Reference Codes	Grade Levels
1. Decisions — Open-Chair Brainstorm (once per month)	HV, pp. 171-175	9-12
2. Marijuana Story	HV, pp. 180-183	7-12
3. Medical Autopsy	GIT, pp. 146-147	7-12
4. Acceptable and Unacceptable Alternatives	D (LG), p. 25 D, p. 26	9-12
5. Risk Taking: It Happens Every Day	D (LG), p. 30 D, p. 35	9-12
6. Choosing from Probabilities	D (LG), pp. 30-31 D, p. 36	9-12
7. An Illustration of Risk Taking: Which Course to Take?	D (LG), p. 31 D, p. 37	9-12
8. Personality and Risk-Taking	D (LG), p. 31-32 D, pp. 38-39	9-12
9. Choosing a Job: An Experiment	D (LG), pp. 32-33 D, p. 40	9-13
10. Decision-Making Strategies	D (LG) pp. 33-34 D, pp. 41-42	9-12
11. Testing Yourself on Strategy	D (LG), pp. 34-35 D, p. 43	9-12
12. Identifying Strategies	D (LG), pp. 35-36 D, p. 44	9-12

Resource Activities*	Reference Codes	Grade Levels
13. Other Types of Decision-Making Strategies	D (LG), p. 36 D, pp. 44-45	9-12
14. Decision-Agent Role Play	RP, pp. 94-97	9-12
15. The Tibetan Monk	RP, p. 160	9-12
16. The Heinze Dilemma	RP, pp. 160-162	9-12
17. "Lost on the Moon — " A Group Consensus Task	UYO, pp. 104-105	7-12
18. Kidney Machine	PE, pp. 243-245	7-12

*See Appendix B.

GOAL V

To Improve Coping Ability

The goal of coping encompasses a multiplicity of behaviors and skills invoked by individuals to meet the internal and external demands of various environments. Burgeoning adolescents often find themselves in the predicament of having to assume new and sometimes contradictory roles in the presence of peers, adults, and authority figures in order to cope with the expectations of different social contexts. They are subject to criticism, competitiveness, and rigid requirements, all of which produce frustration, stress, and anxiety.

The eight objectives, designed to address these issues, run parallel to each other and the sequence you choose will depend on your assessment of students' needs. Use self-report and observation instruments listed in Appendix C to gather data.

The exercises and behavioral management techniques in this section are for both groups and individuals. Here are the means to handle stress and frustration, to approach demanding tasks, and to assume role behaviors without losing personal integrity.

In leading these activities, you should express clearly their rationales and purposes. Your participation should help to relieve the inhibitions of others. Brainstorming is useful here. Careful questioning about such issues as the effects of others' expectations, the difficulties in playing different roles, and the problems in recognizing personal stress are instrumental to the effectiveness of the exercises. When using the self-management approaches, be sure to monitor each student's progress regularly.

103

OBJECTIVE 1

TO TOLERATE COMPETITION WITHIN AND BETWEEN GROUPS

STRATEGIES

1. Non-Verbal Activities

    Divide students into small groups to complete non-verbal curriculum-related activities in a given time. No talking is allowed. Stress the rules that talkers are disqualified and that all communication must be performed by gestures, signs, notes, and other non-verbal expressions. Sample activities might include puzzles, collages, or models of cities related to the curriculum. Acknowledge groups as they complete their activities. Then discuss how each group felt as they competed to finish the tasks within the time limit.

2. Task Groups

    Assign students to small compatible groups to complete reading, social studies, or other assignments posing problems. Establish a time limit. Each group is to develop solutions to the problems. They will be graded on both the content and rationale for solutions. A group spokesperson will report on how the members helped each other to complete the tasks and solve the problems.

    While the individuals in each group will cooperate, the groups compete against each other to become more cohesive and competent. Discuss the ways in which the competition between groups affected the process.

3. Relay Race

    Divide students into groups of six to eight members. After moving desks, chairs, and obstructions to the side of the room, stage a relay race. The object of the race is for each participant to carry a dry sponge, card, or other object on his or her head from a start line to a finish line. Participants from each group take turns walking from start to finish line. After reaching the finish, the participant brings the sponge back to the start line and hands it to the next carrier. If a player drops the sponge, he or she must return to the start line and begin again. The team that finishes first wins the relay race. If your group is large, you may need to appoint referees to enforce the rules.

After the race is over, discuss the following questions:

1. What was it like for you to be racing against the other groups?
2. Were any of your competitors personal friends?
3. If your group was losing, did its slow members get blamed? What comments were made?
4. Did your group have a hero? What kind of feedback did the hero receive?
5. Were differences observed between the boys and girls? Were they treated differently by team members?

Resource Activities*	Reference Codes	Grade Levels
1. Broken Squares	HB I, pp. 25-29	7-12
2. Model Building	HB II, pp. 29-31	7-12
3. Wooden Blocks	HB IV, pp. 18-20	7-12
4. Riddles	HB V, pp. 5-7	9-12
5. Pins and Straws	HB V, pp. 78-84	7-12
6. Examining Non-Verbal Behavior	DAE, pp. 67-69	7-12
7. Conflict Scavenger Hunt	DAE, pp. 294-295	7-12
8. General Instructional Game Structure	LTA, pp. 87-90	7-12
9. Teaching-Role Checklist for Competition Instruction	LTA, pp. 125-127	7-12
10. Marble-Pull Exercise	LTA, pp. 200-202	7-8
11. Choice Cards Exercise	LTA, pp. 202-203	7-9
12. Caterpillar Race	ICE, pp. 17-18	2-12
13. Printed Foot Race	ICE, pp. 55-56	7-12
14. The Welsh Boothouse	DHR, pp. 67-69	10-12

*See Appendix B.

OBJECTIVE 2

TO COMPLETE ASSIGNMENTS WITHIN GIVEN TIME LIMITS

STRATEGIES

1. Time Record

    Ask students to keep record sheets on the week's homework assignments. A sample follows:

Name _____	Date _____	
Subject	*Assignment*	*Time Required*
1. _____	_____	_____
2. _____	_____	_____
3. _____	_____	_____

Review the records weekly and ask students to write statements describing how to make more efficient use of their time. Adapt new techniques and start a new schedule for each week.

2. Time Economy Improvement

Have students record task completion times for similar tasks each week; chart and compare. Chart progress on bar graph.

Example:

Name: _____

Task: _____ Written Definitions of Ten Words _____

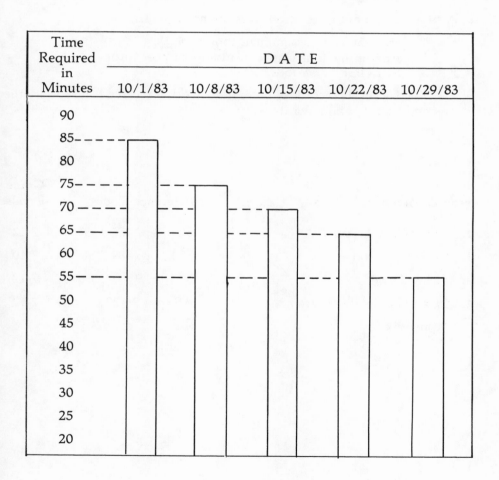

Students should aim to reduce task completion times by at least ten minutes each week. Remind students not to sacrifice quality work for speed.

3. Homework Incentive Program

   To improve students' motivation to complete homework on schedule, set up an incentive program. Include a reward system and schedule in your grading method. Each assignment turned in on time and accurately completed results in extra privileges, credits or requirement waivers.

   At the middle school level, incentives might include the following:

   1. Tokens such as 45 RPM records or rock posters.
   2. Privileges including delivering messages or extra break time.
   3. Options for different homework assignments.

   At the high school level, incentives might include:

   1. Free choice of assignment topics.
   2. Appointment as class consultants or peer tutors.
   3. Extra library periods.

   Keep accurate records of dates homework is received and specify the preconditions for all rewards.

Resource Activities*	Reference Codes	Grade Levels
1. Vocabulary Lesson	SCL, pp. 155-165	7-12
2. Comma Lesson	SCL, pp. 189-209	7-10
3. Straw Tower	NM, p. 9	7-12
4. I Can Handle It My Way	AB, pp. 26-27	7-12

*See Appendix B.

OBJECTIVE 3

TO RECOGNIZE REALISTIC ABILITIES AND LIMITATIONS

STRATEGIES

1. Behavior Chart

    Use this technique to develop realistic self-appraisal and improvement programs by having students chart their behavior on a weekly basis. Each day, negative or positive behavior is recorded and the student charts it to see his or her improvement.

    Some behaviors to improve upon might include:

    1. School attendance

    2. Homework completion

    3. Being influenced by peers to do the wrong thing

    4. Time management and procrastination

    5. Development of hobbies

    6. Faithfulness to friends or relatives

    7. Hygiene habits

    8. Health and diet habits

    9. Temper control

    10. Relaxation techniques

    11. Exercise routines

    12. Spiritual or religious activities

    13. Entertainment activities

    14. Reading

    15. Instrumental music

Example:

Name: _____

Behavior: Asking relevant questions in history class

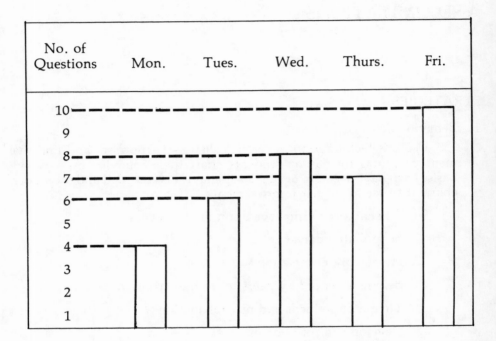

2. Goal Advisors

Encourage students to formulate one specific academic or personal goal every marking period. Then have them develop a list of ways in which they will attempt to accomplish the goal. Encourage them to choose a peer partner with whom they feel comfortable to exchange goals and monitor each other's progress. Input from partners should include judgments about the attainability of the goals that are chosen.

3. Grade Yourself

Ask students to assign grades to their assignments. Have them compare their grades with your grades and chart the differences at regular intervals. Encourage students to develop lists of criteria they use to arrive at their grades.

Make it clear that, as the teacher, your marks are the official standard, but give students the opportunity to confer with you. This process may sharpen their critical thinking, assessment, and negotiation skills. A sample of a typical profile appears below:

| Name: _____ | Grade: 10 | Class: English |

Assignment

Grades	Book Report		Research Project		Composition		Vocabulary Test	
	Teacher	Student	Teacher	Student	Teacher	Student	Teacher	Student
100								
90								
80								
70								
60								
50								
40								
30								
20								
10								
0								
Dates	9/10		10/4		10/15		11/1	

4. Visual Power

    To help students overcome fears about upcoming challenges, encourage them to use the visualization technique below.

    Try to neutralize negative feelings about an upcoming challenge. Use a previous power state scenario to cover up an image of a negative situation that evokes stress. Move the positive scene over the challenging scene very slowly, till it covers over the negative image. This technique can do a lot to take the edge off a challenging situation.

Resource Activities*	Reference Codes	Grade Levels
1. Hopes	HV, pp. 90-91	7-12
2. How Obsessive-Compulsive Are You?	UYO, p. 63	9-12
3. How Shy Are You?	UYO, pp. 64-65	9-12

*See Appendix B.

OBJECTIVE 4

TO RESPOND APPROPRIATELY TO HOSTILITY AND CRITICISM FROM OTHERS

STRATEGIES

1. Verbal Abuse and Criticism

   Engage the class in discussion of how students become scapegoats and suggest ways to manage the anxiety produced by verbal aggression. List ways to react to derogatory attacks. Ask students to compare their reactions to destructive versus constructive criticism. In the discussion try to determine why people like to make fun of others, what purpose such attacks serve, and what they lead to.

2. The Instant Turn-Off

   Use this exercise to demonstrate how people can turn off others who voice criticism and hostility. Have the group observe a role-played conversation between yourself and a student during which the student criticizes your teaching techniques. Instead of responding to the criticism, tune it out and fantasize about where you would like to be at that moment. Then respond to the student by describing what it is like to be in your special place. Include both the setting and the action, such as a fantasy of yourself at a concert, on a quiet beach, or any other pleasant setting.

   Lead a discussion on how people may wander into their own world to avoid facing the reality of someone else's nagging or demands.

   The second step involves having the group form pairs and spend five minutes role-playing dialogues in which one student provokes while the other tunes out and responds by sharing his or her fantasy. After five minutes, ask the students to reverse roles.

   Repeat the exercise a third time, encouraging the responders to face the situation and reply with their honest reactions to criticism and hostility. Discuss the ways we use fantasy to escape the pain of devaluation.

113

3. Reflective Criticsm

   Introduce this exercise by asking the students to recall situations when they were being justly criticized. Encourage students to reflect on how they often secretly agreed with the criticism but could not admit it. Then ask them to write down one critical comment about themselves. Divide the group into pairs and ask partners to trade their critical comments. Provide the following instructions:

   > Read each other's items. Then assume roles as "speakers" and "receivers." The receiver gives the speaker his written self-criticism. Then the speaker states the parner's self-criticism in two ways: face the receiver as if you were actually criticizing him or her; for example if your partner mentioned poor handwriting as a weakness, the speaker says, "You have terrible handwriting."
   >
   > After hearing the first critical statement, the receiver responds by saying how he or she feels, paying attention to *how* the statement was spoken and what emotions it evoked. Then the speaker repeats the same comment, but this time the receiver responds only to the *contents* of the statement. Then switch roles and try the same sequence again.

   After about ten minutes, call the group together for a discussion. Emphasize how painful it is to be criticized and how difficult it is to hear the actual message and evaluate its meaning. Illuminate how the focus often shifts to the emotional tone instead of the actual message.

Resource Activities*	Reference Codes	Grade Levels
1. Solving Human Relations Problems in the Personalized Classroom	PE, pp. 60-64	7-12
2. Fall-Out Shelter Problem	VC, pp. 281-286	7-12
3. Lost on the Moon: A Group Consensus Task	UYO, pp. 104-105	7-12
4. Marijuana Story	HV, pp. 180-183	7-12
5. Let Off Steam	LHT, pp. 97-98	7-12
6. The Portrait Game	HB IV, pp. 24-26	7-12
7. Hands Game (I)	AG, p. 51	7-12

*See Appendix B.

OBJECTIVE 5

TO DEAL WITH SCHOOL'S DISCIPLINE REQUIREMENTS

STRATEGIES

1. Posted Standards of Behavior

    To indicate clear parameters of acceptable behavior, post a short list of expected standards of conduct in the room together with the consequences of flagrant deviations. Install a system whereby positive behaviors result in extra credit assignments of the students' choice.

2. Class Meetings

    Hold periodic meetings to enable students to discuss their concerns about the discipline requirements of the class. Encourage members to brainstorm potential sources of conflict and develop guidelines to deal with them. Always clarify and list the classroom behavior codes, making copies available to the entire group.

3. Moving Close to Students

    Move close to students whose attention appears to wander during group activities. You may also guide the wanderers back to the task by asking more attentive students to form pairs with them. The attentive partners provide behavioral cues to assist in monitoring the inattentive student.

4. Critical Commentaries

    Ask your group to focus on the school's "hot issues" through expressive writing by assigning compositions about school or community problems that impact on their lives. Such issues might include: school vandalism and theft, school rules or police behavior.

    Ask them to analyze the whys and wherefores of these problems, pose solutions, and describe what they reflect about the people concerned. Discuss the writings and reflections with the group.

Resource Activities*	Reference Codes	Grade Levels
1. Boxed-In	BVC, pp. 124-126	7-12
2. How School Groups Control You	NM, p. 60	9-12
3. Looking at School Controls	NM, p. 61	9-12
4. School Manual	NM, p. 62	9-12
5. The School Controlling Itself	NM, p. 63	9-12
6. The Ten Commandments	DHP II, p. 29	7-12
7. Needs and Responsibilities Cards	DHP II, pp. 30-31	7-12
8. Needs and Responsibilities Worksheets	DHP II, pp. 31-32	7-12
9. Petitions	PE, pp. 224-226	7-12

*See Appendix B.

OBJECTIVE 6

TO USE INNER CONTROLS TO PROMOTE RESPONSES OTHER THAN IMPULSIVE BEHAVIOR

STRATEGIES

1. Selective Validation

   To encourage students to learn classroom behavioral skills, try this technique. Rather than reprimanding students who call out instead of raising their hands when responding to questions, ignore their impulsive acts. Instead accept answers to questions only from a student whose hand is raised. Then recognize and encourage participation.

   Counseling group leaders should instruct group members to respond only to peers who speak without interrupting others. Set up a structure which promotes appropriate controls by encouraging group members to ignore inappropriate outbursts and respond to those members who listen to others.

2. Impulse Search[32]

   Define the word "impulse" for the group. Ask students to describe some impulses and desires that are at times hard to control. List and distribute examples, then brainstorm potential techniques to control the kind of behavior which often leads to trouble. Use the list to enable students to become aware of typical outbursts and ways to monitor their behavior.

[32]This strategy was developed by Michael Villano, chairman, Social Studies Department, Fort Lee High School, Fort Lee, N.J. Adapted by permission of the author.

3. Response Notebook[33]

   Approach the student with an impulse control problem by having him or her keep a special notebook for use during problem situations. Notebooks should have pre-printed pages like the following example.

Example:

Comment or Question	
Time	
Date	
Response Checklist	**Response Choices**
	1. Can answer it myself.
	2. Can wait until the end of class.
	3. Can wait until speaker is finished, and teacher is not busy.
	4. Requires immediate attention.

During times of increased activity, impulsive students are asked to jot down the comment or question they wish to present, and check the appropriate response column *before speaking or acting out behavior.* Student and teacher review and discuss notebook recordings at end of the day. Teacher praises checks in "Can answer it myself" and "Can wait" columns. Student and teacher propose appropriate ways of responding when the situation "requires immediate attention," i.e., use of a special minimally disruptive student-teacher cue or signal.

Discuss impulsive and non-impulsive responses in an effort to generate alternative behaviors. Goals can be set for obtaining more "Can answer it myself" and "Can wait" checks, along with an appropriate reward or recognition system.

4. Reactions to Gifts

As you approach Christmas and Hanukkah Holidays, hold a discussion on giving and receiving. Ask the members to imagine receiving gifts that they really did not appreciate and have them discuss their reactions.

Then ask the group to develop a list of various acceptable reactions to gifts and their givers.

33This strategy was developed by Carolyn Kehayan, special education teacher, Fort Lee Public Schools, Fort Lee, N.J. Used by permission of the author.

5. Positive Posture

To help students overcome fears about upcoming challenges, encourage them to use the visualization technique below.

Visualize and experience a positive state you were in, when you had it all together. Imagine yourself being in the scene. Notice the posture you were in as you were experiencing the positive state. Try to move yourself into the same posture. Change your breathing to match the power state. Also change the way you are moving to match the power state. You will be surprised how much your physical state can change your mental state from a negative to a positive mode.

6. Negative Commands

Negative commands can be very helpful in dealing with someone who tends to be oppositional. There are a lot of people who take great pleasure in contradicting and questioning whatever you say. When trying to assist someone who is oppositional, you may want to preface your remarks negatively. The stubborn person who needs to change his antagonistic behavior might respond well to a statement such as, "You don't want to control your outburst until you're ready." Another example would be a remark to someone who wishes to lose weight, "Don't stop eating until you're ready to be very thin."

The negative command principle can have disastrous impact if used in the wrong way. For example, using negative commands to stop behavior can only reinforce it. When someone is talking too loud you might want them to quiet down and say, "Don't talk so loud." They will have difficulty stopping because the real message is, "talk loud." Saying "Be quiet" is much more useful.

Resource Activities*	Reference Codes	Grade Levels
1. Dental Aggression	NM, p. 76	9-12
2. Board of Directors	NM, p. 76	9-12
3. Consequences of My Actions	PE, pp. 293-294	9-12
4. Working with Obstacles	GFF, pp. 141-142	9-12
5. Working Objectively to Explore Emotion	GFF, pp. 187-188	9-12
6. What Did They Solve?	AB, pp. 31-33	7-12

*See Appendix B.

OBJECTIVE 7

TO COPE WITH STRESS AND FRUSTRATING EXPERIENCES

STRATEGIES

1. Unloading Baggage

   To promote a better understanding of how people deal with stress, anger, and unwanted feelings, try this technique.

   Donate an old, empty briefcase or canvas bag and ask the group to fill it (over a period of a week) with anonymously written paragraphs describing criticism, annoyance, frustration, dislikes, and other negative "emotional baggage" from stressful experiences.

   Each week discuss the group's common denominators, possible solutions, and vehicles to initiate positive changes.

2. Over the Edge[34]

   Discuss with the class how certain personal crises cause one to feel enormous stress and pressure. Ask the group to list specific situations which can bring one to say, "If this keeps up, I'll go nuts."

   Then lead a discussion about high stress situations to identify common stressors and potential ways to cope with them.

---

[34]This strategy was suggested by Michael Villano, chairman, Social Studies Department, Fort Lee High School, Fort Lee, N.J. Used by permission of the author.

120

3. The Major Exam[35]

To capture the terror often experienced by students taking exams, set up a highly-structured simulated testing situation without previous preparation. Ask the class to clear their desks, move them away from each other, and take out their pens or pencils.

Make up and distribute a test and answer sheet with detailed instructions. Set a time limit. Inform the group that they will be graded on accuracy, ability to follow directions, grammar, and spelling. No talking is allowed. Students should not turn toward others or leave their seats until the time period is over.

After the exam is finished, initiate a discussion to deal with the following issues:

1. Personal reactions to the exam.
2. Fears about failure.
3. Impact of these feelings on their ability to perform.
4. Strategies employed by students to remain calm, keep working, and finish the exam.

Follow up with additional brainstorming activity to generate coping strategies which may be passed along to the class to use during subsequent testing situations.

[35]This strategy was developed by Marcia Wyrtzen, staff therapist, Center for Creative Living, Allendale, N.J. and by Linda Max De Sheplo. Used by permission of the authors.

4. Stress Conditions and Warning Signals

    Ask students to use this check list to identify those conditions and warning signals which are impacting their lives.

    Distribute Stress Conditions Sheets and Internal Warning Signal Check Lists. Allow ten minutes for the group to read silently through them. Hold a large group discussion of how the condition reactions impact the trainees in their own lives. Be sure to allow members to "pass" on personal information that is too threatening or painful to share publicly.

    Make sure you emphasize the need to check out any physical symptoms with a physician before assuming they are just stress reactions.

Stress Conditions

_____ Loss of special person	_____ Parent substance abuse
_____ Poor grades	_____ Conflict with opposite sex
_____ Parent pressure	
_____ Peer pressure	_____ Family problem
_____ Physical changes	_____ Teenage pregnancy
_____ Parental divorce or separation	_____ Personal substance abuse
_____ Fears about future	_____ Social anxiety
_____ Lack of friends	_____ Financial trouble
_____ Loss of job	_____ Overload

Permission to reprint Copyright © 1990, V. Alex Kehayan, _Self-Awareness Growth Experiences_, Jalmar Press, Rolling Hills Estates, CA.

Internal Warning Signals Check List

Goal: To identify your personal warning signals of stress.

Directions: Use this check list to identify personal warning signals of stress impacting your life.

_____ Cold hands	_____ Stomach problems
_____ Fast breathing	_____ Diarrhea
_____ Sweaty hands	_____ Frequent urination
_____ Muscle tension	_____ Sleep disturbances
_____ Furrowed brow	_____ Irritability
_____ Tremors or tics	_____ Headaches
_____ Panic attacks	_____ Sadness
_____ Anxious feelings	_____ Apathy
_____ Blushing	_____ Impatience
_____ High blood pressure	_____ Phobias
_____ Non-medical physical symptoms	_____ Respiratory problems
_____ Feeling disconnected from life	_____ Drinking or drugs
_____ Distractible	_____ Plagued by repetitious thoughts
_____ Short tempered	_____ Suicidal thoughts

Permission to reprint: Copyright © 1990, V. Alex Kehayan, *Self-Awareness Growth Experiences*, Jalmar Press, Rolling Hills Estates, CA.

Go to bed to sleep, not to worry. If you are stressed, get up and read a book, watch TV, etc.

If you can't sleep, try this exercise: Imagine yourself at a chalkboard with a tray next to it. Imagine that on the try is a piece of chalk and an eraser. Imagine yourself picking up the chalk, reaching out to the board, and writing the number 100. Then slowly bring your arm down to the tray, leave the chalk, and pick up the eraser. Lift the eraser slowly to the board and erase the 100. Then slowly bring the eraser down to the tray, pick up the chalk again and move it to the board. Write the number 99, and continue slowly. Drop one number each time you run through the cycle.

Avoid self-medication, taking tranquilizers, drinking, or using any other substances.

Take a break and move to another location to interrupt the stress pattern.

Set goals that are within your reach.

Beware of attempting to control situations that are totally out of your control. Instead, practice ways of dealing with them more effectively.

Use tension outlets that work for you such as exercise, pillow fights, screaming, writing in a journal, etc. Make sure these outlets don't produce more stress.

Schedule regular talk time to clear the air with high stress producing individuals.

Call your friends to get support.

See a funny movie, talk to a funny person, read a funny story, think of a funny experience.

Use hobbies, sports, and artistic outlets.

Practice deep breathing low in the abdomen. Move your breath slowly downward, deepening each breath and lengthening to intervals. Imagine pure air coming into your lungs, cleansing your mind.

For a headache, pretend to surround the area of pain with a rubber band. Gradually stretch the rubber band very slowly, moving the pain, down your arms, into your fingers, and out your fingernails. Do this in slow motion, breathing deeply from the abdomen, with every breath making the pain thinner and weaker, as it flows out your body.

Visualize a calm scene with all the colors and sounds and sights. Imagine yourself being in the scene and run it in slow motion until you get to the most enjoyable part. Then step into the picture.

Use symbols to connect with the most relaxing experiences or inner state.

Try listening to your favorite music and making up new lyrics that guide you through a difficult situation. "I'm going to make it through this mess, the way I did last time..." It sounds silly but it will work with the more light-hearted person.

Resource Activities*	Reference Codes	Grade Levels
1. Assessing Your Interpersonal Stress	UYO, pp. 69-71	9-12
2. Learning to Relax	UYO, pp. 81-82	9-12
3. Desensitizing Yourself to Stressful Situations	UYO, p. 89	9-12
4. Working with Obstacles (I)	GFF, pp. 141-142	7-12
5. Relaxation (I)	GFF, pp. 148-150	7-12
6. Using Frustration to Stimulate Invention	GFF, pp. 168-169	7-12
7. Breathing	DAE, pp. 79-81	9-12
8. Stretch	DAE, pp. 82-83	9-12
9. Class Applause	100, p. 222	7-12
10. Not Listening	HB III, pp. 10-13	9-12
11. Boxed-In	BVC, pp. 124-126	7-12
12. Silent Scream	LHT, p. 96	7-8
13. Let Off Steam	LHT, pp. 97-98	7-12
14. Frustrating Games	LHT, pp. 102-103	7-12
15. How I relax	ICE, pp. 37-38	7-12

*See Appendix B.

OBJECTIVE 8

TO ATTEND SCHOOL AND CLASSES REGULARLY AND ON TIME

STRATEGIES

1. Attendance Chart

    Request students to keep individual weekly attendance charts. A time graph, such as the one below, is self-reinforcing and can be reviewed periodically. Rewards, such as free time or extra credit opportunities, may be issued to those students who satisfy your prescribed criteria.

Example:

Attendance Chart				
Name:				
Month of:		May		
Days Present	5/1-5/5	5/7-5/11	5/14-5/18	5/20-5/24	5/27-6/1

2. Morning Assistant[36]

As a promptness incentive, assign students with tardiness or attendance problems special responsibilities to be completed 10 to 15 minutes prior to the beginning of the school day. Examples of morning responsibilities might be:

1. Posting the school announcements, joke or quote of the day, or special calendar events on the class bulletin board.
2. Helping the principal, office secretaries, or custodian with preparations for the school day.
3. Monitoring the hallways as students enter the building and go to their lockers.

Tasks should be appealing to the student and deemed important by other pupils and the school staff.

[36]This strategy was developed by Carolyn Kehayan, special education teacher, Fort Lee Public Schools, Fort Lee, N.J. Used by permission of the author.

3. Recognition Bulletin Board[37]

Enlist students to design a bulletin board displaying certificates for gains and achievements made in attendance, classroom behavior, academics, homework, and extra curricular activities.

Students draw the format of the certificates on ditto masters that can be run off. The certificates should include spaces for: student's name, date, school, commendation description, and signatures of teacher, student, and administration. The commendations should be neatly framed with construction paper on cardboard and displayed on the bulletin board for a specified period, then taken home to receive additional recognition from the parents.

Certificates can also be filed in a class Recognition Scrapbook or in an individual student's certificate folder.

[37]This strategy was developed by Carolyn Kehayan, special education teacher, Fort Lee Public Schools, Fort Lee, N.J. Used by permission of the author.

Resource Activity*	Reference Codes	Grade Levels
1. Tardy Employees	CGG, p. 61	7-12

*See Appendix B.

GOAL VI

To Develop
Ethical Standards

We are currently flooded with ethical and moral issues encompassing such profound areas as sexual morality, political scandals, media control over accurate information, and double standards in business, to name a few. The basic ethical teachings promoted by our schools carry the same paradoxes and controversies that exist in society at large.

The purpose of this section is to provide a humanistic approach to the ethical issues faced by young people who constantly experience conflict when forced to choose between morally toned behaviors and to accept the consequences of their actions. This goal's basic assumption is that students should conform to self-imposed, humanistic standards of behavior in their quest for internal equilibrium and the alleviation of guilt.

Among the universal values presented in this section are truthfulness, acceptance of responsibility, and fairness to others. The exercises and events are designed to simulate moral dilemmas and provide opportunities to experience the feelings, consequences, and feedback of others. Adolescents often find it difficult to move out of the conformity-oriented level of morality. Kohlberg (1971) terms this level The Conventional Stage. Therefore, the focus here is to enable students to reach more internalized, universally oriented levels of moral development.

The three objectives are parallel and do not require a specific sequence. Use your assessments, behavioral observations, and student input to guide you in selecting objectives for each student. When leading the activities and events, be aware of your own moral principles and guard against inculcation. Attempt to provide opportunities for students to discuss and compare moral values emerging from their own behavior. Equanimity, free expression, and acceptance of the morality of others should guide you toward responsible leadership.

131

OBJECTIVE 1

TO TAKE RESPONSIBILITY FOR ACTIONS INSTEAD OF BLAMING OTHERS OR EXTERNAL CIRCUMSTANCES

STRATEGIES

1. Who's to Blame?[38]

   Distribute copies of the following story and read it aloud to the group. Then initiate a discussion to discover and explore personal attitudes about responsibility and blame as they apply to interpersonal relationships.

   Who's to Blame?

   Ron and Debbie attend the same high school and have known each other since elementary school. They have been going out for two years. Debbie has been spending much time with Ron, and looks forward to his frequent phone calls. She has a few close friends and sees them at cheer-leading activities, school clubs and other in-school events. After school time and weekends have been devoted exclusively to seeing Ron.

   Ron has a few friends but rarely sees them after school. His friends are gradually disowning him because they resent all the time he spends with Debbie. One day after school he meets Debbie and announces that he no longer intends to spend Saturdays and Sundays with her. He explains that his valuable friendships are too important to lose. Debbie is very upset and hurt. The next day she sees Ron's friends in school and tells them off. Ron finds out and becomes very angry with her for interfering with his friendships. They have a serious falling-out and their relationship is ruined.

   Ask the students to list the characters on a sheet of paper in order of their preferences, from most to least admired. Lead a lively discussion in which group members are asked to explain their preferences. The implications of each character's actions should raise questions and facilitate dialogues about the origins of blame and denial of personal responsibility.

---

[38]This strategy was developed collaboratively by Carolyn Kehayan, special education teacher, Fort Lee Public Schools, Fort Lee, N.J. and the author. Used by permission.

2. The Spotlight Game[39]

This event requires materials and advance preparation. You will need a flashlight, oaktag, string, and magic markers. Make up several signs (with strings attached) to illustrate how people take the emphasis off themselves and place it on others. Some guidelines for signs are given below.

Front Side	Reverse Side
Lazy	I am worried that I don't do enough with my abilities.
Slob	I feel uncomfortable about my own cleanliness and bad habits.
Cool	I am worried about my image and I envy you.
Ugly	I am concerned about my appearance.
Fag	I am concerned about my own masculinity or femininity.
Retard	You are not learning and I can't figure out why. It makes me feel like a poor teacher or parent.

Introduce this exercise by dimming the lights, holding a lighted flashlight, and discussing the feelings invoked by the "imaginary audience" fantasy. Proceed as follows:

"How many times have you wondered what people around you are thinking about you?" (Pause) Point the flashlight at yourself as you ask, "How many times have you ever felt like you were in the spotlight and sensed the pressure of others staring at you?" Someone is probably saying, "He has bad breath." (Pause) Then point the flashlight at someone else while saying, "No, I don't have bad breath; you do." Explain that the easiest way to get yourself out of the spotlight is to put it one someone else."

Then ask the group, "How many of you have ever been called a name by others?" Ask students if they have ever heard these names used by others: "Lazy." (Pause) "Slob." (Pause) "Cool." (Pause) "Ugly." (Pause) "Fag." (Pause) "Retard." As the hands go up for each name you call, hang the appropriate sign on one student until all the signs are given out. Then raise the lights and ask each student to read aloud the label on the front and the real message on the back.

Engage the class in a discussion about how people use degrading labels to take the emphasis off themselves and place it on others. You may want to ask the students to make up additional signs for other labels and personal concerns.

[39]This strategy was developed by James Warnke, M.S.W., psychotherapist, Teaneck, N.J. Used by permission of the author.

3. To Blame or Not to Blame[40]

This strategy requires some advance preparation and arrangements with other teachers.

Ask high school students to write hypothetical stories about a middle school boy or girl who encounters social and academic difficulties during the seventh and eighth grades. The stories should focus on how this seventh- or eighth-grader blames other people and situations for his or her problems. Writers should draw on their own experiences to help them portray realistic situations to which middle school students can relate.

Completed stories are mailed to selected seventh- and eighth-graders who read the story and jot down ways that the character could resolve the problems without blaming others. These suggestions are returned to the high school authors who evaluate and write comments on the proposed solutions. (Encourage high school students to give positive and constructive feedback in their commentaries.) Then the stories and comments are returned to the younger pupils.

Note: This exercise may lead to ongoing pen pal relationships between high school and middle school students.

Resource Activities*	Reference Codes	Grade Levels
1. Do You Perceive Yourself as an Origin or a Pawn?	UYO, pp. 61-62	9-12
2. Responsibility	DAE, pp. 87-88	10-12
3. Consequences of Your Actions	PE, pp. 293-294	7-12
4. Responsibility Pie	DHP, p. 25	7-12
5. Needs and Responsibilities Cards	DHP II, pp. 30-31	7-12
6. Needs and Responsibilities Worksheets	DHP II, pp. 31-32	7-12
7. Self-Sabotage Role Play	DHP II, pp. 34-35	7-12
8. Responsibilities Lifeline	DHP II, pp. 36-37	7-12

*See Appendix B.

[40]This strategy was developed by Carolyn Kehayan, special education teacher, Fort Lee Public Schools, Fort Lee, N.J. Used by permission of the author.

OBJECTIVE 2

TO COMPETE FAIRLY

STRATEGIES

1. Timed Group Projects

Break the class into three groups and assign each group the same task, i.e., a mathematics equation or crossword puzzle. Set a time limit for the task.

Then require each group to formulate its own rules for behavior and participation in the problem-solving process. Ask members to assume roles as secretary, computer, checker, monitor of rules, and spokesperson. The secretary records program notes. The computer solves the mathematics problem or crossword puzzle, and the checker reviews the work for accuracy. The rules monitor observes the process, enforces the guidelines, and deals with members who break rules. The spokesperson reports the outcomes to the larger group.

Reward the first group to finish the task successfully. Discuss some of the issues of cooperation and fair play that emerged through the exercise.

2. Change the Rules

Have playing cards and board games on hand. Ask students to form small groups of three or four members.

Assign one member of each group to play the role of "leader." The other members are "players" who must follow the leader's directives. Distribute the games to each group.

Instruct the groups as follows:

This is an exercise designed to allow you to play a game. Remember when you were very young and wanted desperately to win a game? And, when you were losing, you wished you could change the rules to give you the advantage. Did you ever play checkers, for example, and change the rules to allow kings to jump their own men?

Well, now you are going to get your chance to play a game and announce a rules change when it serves your needs. Each of you will have five minutes to be a leader with the right to change the rules whenever you feel like it. The other players must follow your rules.

After each five-minute time frame, signal the groups to change leaders until all participants have been leaders.

After everyone has had a turn, lead a short discussion illuminating the various reactions to the leaders who changed rules. Ask about the consequences of recurrent changes in rules and their impact on the order, clarity, and justice in actual life situations.

3. Catch the Cheater[41]

This event requires some advance preparation. Make arrangements with an elementary classroom teacher to visit his or her class for two periods. Then instruct students in your group to bring in some board games borrowed from younger siblings. Take the group to an elementary class and have them form groups of four.

Ask the elementary students to surround and observe each group while they spend twenty minutes playing a game. Instruct the players to attempt to break the rules while elementary students observe the process and serve as referees. When elementary student observers notice rule infractions, they must stop the action and call for a replay.

After twenty minutes, form a large group and discuss the merits of fair play and the feelings evoked when cheating occurs.

[41]This strategy was developed collaboratively by Carolyn Kehayan, special education teacher, Fort Lee Public Schools, Fort Lee, N.J. and this author. Used by permission of the author.

Resource Activities*	Reference Codes	Grade Levels
1. Tinkertoy Bridge	HB V, pp. 60-72	9-12
2. The Math Test	GIT, pp. 96-97	7-12
3. The Yahtzee Game	GIT, p. 113	7-9
4. Buying the Boat	GIT, pp. 117-118	7-12
5. TV "News"	GIT, pp. 122-123	7-12
6. Caterpillar Race	ICE, pp. 17-18	7-12

*See Appendix B.

OBJECTIVE 3

TO RESPECT INDIVIDUAL DIFFERENCES WITHOUT STIGMATIZING OTHERS

STRATEGIES

1. Reading in Reverse[42]

    Ask the group to try this experiment to experience the feelings of a person with a learning disability.

    Have them read the following paragraph written backwards and to sign their names on the page using their non-dominant hands. Brief one group member in advance to prepare to read the paragraph with perfect fluency in front of the class.

    After the group has struggled to read for ten minutes, call forth the "confederate" to give a swift, polished reading.

    [42]This strategy was developed by Eileen Garner, special education teacher, Fort Lee High School, Fort Lee, N.J. Used by permission of the author.

Model Paragraph

"A doog, dilos thgie sruoh peels" si debircserp rof gnihtyreve morf noitsuahxe dna nekcihc xop ot ehcatraeh. teY tahw yltcaxe sneppah gnirud esoht thgie sruoh? oD ruo sniarb dna seidob ylpmis deen ot eb "denrut ffo," ekil na revo detaeh enigne, rof a driht fo ruo sevil? dnA tahw tuoba smaerd — did duerF llet su lla ew deen ot wonk tuoba meht?

_____

Signature of student

Disclose the "sting" and then discuss the frustrations of being handicapped and the attendant feelings, struggles, and reactions experienced by handicapped people. Discuss group members' assumptions about learning disabled pupils in the school.

2. Ideal Mates[43]

This event is designed to sensitize students to the needs and stereotypical responses of each gender. Explain that most people have preconceived notions about the ideal girl or boy in their lives. Introduce this exercise as a vehicle to explore fantasies about the opposite sex.

Divide students into small groups and distribute popular teenage magazines. Ask the boys to select pictures of the "dream girls" and the girls to choose "dream boys." Then hold a discussion during which boys describe their dream girls and the girls describe their dream boys.

As a follow-up activity, spend another period examining how the genders perceive each others' ideal qualities. Divide the students into groups of four, each containing two girls and two boys. Ask them to compare and contrast how boys and girls perceive their romantic ideals. Highlight comparable and contrasting perceptions during the discussion.

3. The Foreign Student[44]

Divide the group into several subgroups. One member of each group is to pretend to be from a different country, and will speak only gibberish. Assign an activity requiring active participation of all members of the group, for example, a game of softball or scrabble. Students are to pretend not to understand anything said by the "foreigner."

After the activity is completed, discuss the problems that arose. How might it feel to be an outsider or a foreign person faced with an unknown situation? Seek suggestions to help an outsider become familiar with a group process.

[43]This strategy was developed by James Warnke, M.S.W., psychotherapist, Teaneck, N.J. Adapted by permission of the author.

[44]This strategy was developed by Marcia Wyrtzen, staff therapist, Center for Creative Living, Allendale, N.J., and Linda Max De Sheplo. Used by permission of the authors.

4. Struggling with Visual Impairment [45]

This exercise sensitizes the group to the anxiety produced by testing situations.

Without prior preparation, announce that the group is about to receive a graded assignment. Reproduce and distribute the following paragraph and questions. Allow only 15 minutes for students to read the paragraph and to write answers to questions at the end of the story. Most pupils will not finish. Do not allow any talking and do not answer any questions.

Planet 455 [46]

Life on Planet 455 was a series of never-ending conflicts. The Mulkrow Desert people weakened the Nogoosoon fortress by syphoning their fuel supply and depleting their main food source, Pushkin mushrooms. The Yoohoo warriors, situated in temporary space stations, bombarded the planet's wildlife with laser guns in hopes of clearing the land for more permanent settlements. Xion and Rheon tribespeople were driven to surpass one another in armaments while the Rootex continued to bury their radio-active dead near the planet's largest water supply. Because of rising unemployment in Corporate Galactica Bases, unrest among red-buttoned workers persisted. Only the Zephers, who lived quietly beneath the land's middle core, struggled with a more peaceful task: Writing a new constitution that would restore harmony to deteriorating Planet 455.

Comprehension Questions
1. Describe the quality of life on Planet 455.
2. Which two tribespeople were involved in an arms race?
3. Is the water on Planet 455 safe to drink? Why or why not?
4. Which inhabitants seem to be the most peace-loving?
5. Compare life on Planet 455 with life on our planet earth? How is life similar? How is life different?

After the students have worked for 15 minutes discuss the feelings which arose as they struggled to read and comprehend the material in its reduced form. Encourage the group to appreciate the amount of energy required to complete the task and relate this to how blind and partially sighted individuals must struggle to face life in a visually oriented society.

5. An Experience with Disabled People [47]

Organize a trip to a facility for the handicapped or a local festival emphasizing support of the disabled. Your local Association for the Blind, Mental Retardation Society, or Commission on the Handicapped will guide you in your choice of excursion.

Prepare the group by gathering information about and discussing the nature of the particular handicap with which you will be dealing. Encourage discussion on the types of feelings shared by handicapped people and how they expect to be treated. Some group members may have firsthand experience with handicapped individuals in their own family and can be called on to offer valuable information.

[45]This strategy was developed by James Warnke, M.S.W., psychotherapist, Teaneck, N.J. Used by permission of the author.

[46]Planet 455 was written by Carol Kehayan, special education teacher, Fort Lee Public Schools, Fort Lee, N.J. Used by permission of the author.

[47]This strategy was developed by Pat McQuade, special education teacher, Fort Lee High School, Fort Lee, N.J. Used by permission of the author.

A particularly touching experience can be had by visiting a house or school for the mentally retarded during the Christmas Holidays. Many facilities welcome outside help and participation at seasonal parties.

Always follow-up such a visit with a discussion, debriefing, and a brainstorming activity to identify the most sensitive approaches to the disabled.

Resource Activities*	Reference Codes	Grade Levels
1. Males Versus Females: Facts Versus Myths	UYO, p. 1	9-12
2. Perceiving is Believing	UYO, p. 15	9-12
3. Identifying Categories of Prejudice	UYO, p. 137	9-12
4. How to Change Attitudes	UYO, pp. 138-140	9-12
5. Exploring Sex Roles	DHP, pp. 31-32	9-12
6. Prejudice: Identity and Difference	DAE, pp. 94-95	9-12
7. Prejudice: First-Hand Impressions	DAE, pp. 96-97	9-12
8. Male/Female Roles	DAE, pp. 97-102	10-12
9. Group Rejection	DAE, pp. 102-106	7-12
10. Handicapped	DAE, pp. 128-130	10-12
11. Medical Emergency	CGG, p. 26	7-12
12. Boys and Girls	LHT, p. 100	7-8
13. Sensitivity Modules	VC, pp. 266-275	7-12
14. Polarization	HB III, pp. 57-63	9-12

*See Appendix B.

GOAL VII

To Develop Independent Functioning

This section is devoted to enhancing self-regulation and independent functioning, essential qualities for survival in an era fraught with uncertainty, scarcity of resources, and economic instability.

The five objectives are related but not sequentially listed. They are intended to meet the needs of adolescents, struggling with the developmental issues of separation, individuation, and autonomy. The objectives should be chosen on the basis of your observation and careful assessment; and should be addressed in the order determined by student needs.

You will find some individually oriented strategies in this section, which are most applicable to students requiring specific drill and practice in self-management, a skill best learned individually.

Other strategies employ self-exploration — experiential simulations of life situations to foster self-directed behavior. The issues focus on making choices, coping with peer pressure, and examining personal morality. These issues are central to the developmental stage of adolescence. They must be faced, resolved and enhanced before one can move on to develop an autonomous, independent identity based on personal integrity.

It is essential that you point out to your target population the dangers of extreme dependence on "borrowed values" as well as the consequences of totally anarchical behavior. A realistic balance between these two polarities should serve as a guide to implementing the program.

OBJECTIVE 1

TO FOLLOW DIRECTIONS WITHOUT INDIVIDUALIZED ASSISTANCE

STRATEGIES

1. <u>Learning by Verbalizing Instructions</u>[48]

Use the "fading" technique to improve students' ability to interpret and carry out instructions accurately. When using this technique for giving tests or assigning work, it is vital to organize instructions clearly and sequentially.

Give class a preview, such as, "I am going to give you directions on how to do equations. Listen and repeat them." Ask students to repeat and write them in their own words. Encourage students to describe the sequence and avoid parroting the words.

The students then verbalize the instructions as they follow the sequence in doing the equations. In the next step, the students do the equations while whispering or mouthing the instructions. Finally, the students do the equations silently.

[48]This procedure, known as "fading," was developed, described, and implemented by Donald Meichenbaum and Joseph Goodman, and is discussed in "Training Children to Talk to Themselves: A Means of Developing Self-Control," Journal of Abnormal Psychology, Vol. 77, No. 2 (April 1971), pp. 115-126. Adapted by permission of publisher and authors.

2. <u>Color-Coded Directions</u>[49]

When issuing classwork to an individual student who has difficulty following directions, tape a sequential checklist of operations to the pupil's desk. Include squares by each step so that the student can check them off as they are completed. Code key words such as "read," "answer," "write," and "use complete sentences" with contrasting colors to emphasize their importance. Review the process after the student has completed the assignment.

As the student becomes more skilled in following directions, combine operational steps and reduce the number of color-coded words.

3. Write Your Own Directions

When issuing an assignment to a particular student who has difficulty following directions, ask the pupil to develop a list of sequential steps which should be submitted with the completed assignment. Go over the steps with the student and review their sequence and accuracy.

For a book report assignment, a typical sequence might include:

1. Select book.
2. Read and take notes.
3. Identify major themes.
4. Identify major characters and their roles.
5. Develop critical analysis of plots.
6. Outline the report.
7. Write the report.
8. Revise and proofread the report.

Resource Activities*	Reference Codes	Grade Levels
1. Play Ball	HV, pp. 68-71	7-12
2. Independent Study Project Organizer	DHP, pp. 78-79	7-12
3. Student-Designed Learning Program Form	PE, pp. 483-490	7-12
4. Arrange the Cartons	ICE, pp. 340-345	8-12

*See Appendix B.

[49]This strategy was developed by Carolyn Kehayan, special education teacher, Fort Lee Public Schools, Fort Lee, N.J. and the author. Used by permission of the author.

OBJECTIVE 2

TO APPROACH TASKS IN AN ORGANIZED, NON-IMPULSIVE MANNER

STRATEGIES

1. Increased Time Intervals

   Gradually lengthen task activities to provide practice in attaining well-organized approaches to the assignments.

   Example:

   Add two mathematics problems to assignment each week, or add two word definitions to dictionary activities.

   Increase a given task time by ten minutes per week. Ask each student to record when the task is begun and when it is completed.
   Ask the students to chart sustained attention time each week.

Time Chart

Name: _____ Grade: __7__

Subject: __Arithmetic__

Type of Activity: __Two-place multiplication problems__

Date of Assignment	Number of Problems	Time Spent
1/7/83	2	15 minutes
1/17/83	4	17 minutes
1/24/83	6	20 minutes

2. Grade Profile

Have students graph their grades in a particular subject area each week. Check progress periodically.

The following chart is an example of a useful format.

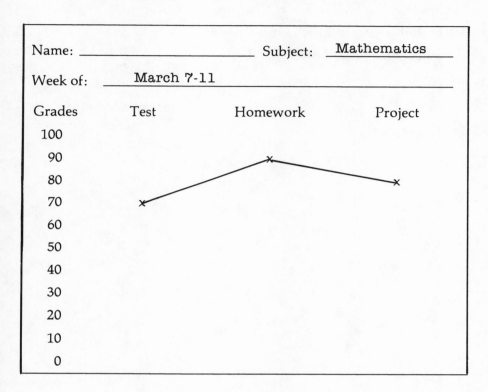

Name: _____ Subject: __Mathematics__

Week of: _____March 7-11_____

Grades	Test	Homework	Project

3. Task Dividing

To get students into an organized routine, break up classwork assignments into three stages and go over each step as you demonstrate the process.

Stage 1: Give directions and clarify for understanding (15 minutes).

Stage 2: Ask class to solve the problem or complete the task (15 minutes).

Stage 3: Review the assignment outcomes and rationales (15 minutes).

Resource Activities*	Reference Codes	Grade Levels
1. Boxed-In	BVC, pp. 124-126	7-12
2. Independent Study Project Organizer	DHP, pp. 78-79	7-12
3. Brainstorming to Reach Organization	HV, p. 139	7-12
4. Student-Designed Learning Program Form	PE, pp. 483-490	7-12
5. Moving in Response to Group Directions	GFF, pp. 139-141	7-12

*See Appendix B.

OBJECTIVE 3

TO USE LEISURE TIME PRODUCTIVELY

STRATEGIES

1. Leisure Time Questions[50]

    Assign the following questions as starting points to generate productive leisure time activities. Ask each student to write an answer to the questions. Collect lists and discuss the leisure time options.

    Suggested Questions

    1. How can you use your time for family and friends?
    2. What are good hobbies to develop?
    3. What hobbies add to the happiness of others?
    4. What can we do to develop good friendships?
    5. What are the possessions that do not cost money nor involve personal investment yet bring to you wealthy dividends of beauty, pleasure, and happiness?

2. Weekend Reflections

    Use the following Feedback Form to promote students' explanation and evaluation of leisure time activities.
    Some of these activities might include:
    1. Social events
    2. Concerts
    3. Hobbies
    4. Sports
    5. Time alone
    6. Shopping
    7. Reading
    8. Watching TV

[50]These questions were developed by Marcia Wrystzen, staff therapist, Center for Creative Living, Allendale, N.J. and Linda Max De Sheplo. Used by permission of the authors.

Feedback Form

Weekend Reflections

1. How satisfied were you with your weekend? (circle one)

   1   2   3   4   5   6   7

   very dissatisfied   very satisfied

2. What do you consider the high point of your weekend?
3. What things gave you satisfaction?
4. What would have made the weekend better?
5. What could friends, parents and others do to make your weekend better?
6. What could you do to make your weekend better?
7. Free comment.

Ask students to write responses to questions in the Feedback Form. Then divide the students into pairs, and have partners exchange their comments and ideas about weekend activities. Use this technique at intervals to note changes in leisure time activities throughout the academic year.

3. Leisure Time Activities Brainstorm

   To explore the use of leisure time and generate new outlets, invite the class to engage in a 15-minute brainstorm on ways to use open time.

   Encourage unconventional uses that spur new hobbies and learning experiences. Help the students identify the activities, their potential for the future, their worth, and their cost. Continue over the weeks to encourage the students to report on their pursuit of new activities. Catalog activities on index cards and place in a Leisure Time file to which students may refer.

Resource Activities*	Reference Codes	Grade Levels
1. Twenty Things You Love to Do	VC, pp. 30-34	7-12
2. The Pie of Life	VC, pp. 228-231	7-12
3. Ready for Summer	VC, pp. 363-365	7-12
4. Values Dilemmas	PE, pp. 254-279	7-12
5. Ways to Spend Free Time	PE, pp. 289-293	7-12

*See Appendix B.

OBJECTIVE 4

TO DEVELOP SELF-MONITORING SKILLS

STRATEGIES

1. Contractual Agreement

   Implement individual contracts such as the one described below (hourly, daily, or weekly, depending on student).

   Contract

   Effective Dates:

   From:_____ To:_____

   This agreement is between_____and_____.
   John Doe agrees to perform the following behaviors:
   1. To attend class on time each day.
   2. To complete homework assignments each week on time.

   In return for which Mr. Thompson will do the following:
   1. Give John Doe a pass for five open-time lunch periods.
   2. Give John Doe a pass to library during five study hall periods

   Agreed: _____ (signed)

   _____ (signed)

   Both sign the agreement. The student, in signing the agreement, agrees to complete each and every assignment. The teacher sets carefully established guidelines. The student should monitor his own progress.

2. Self Management Checklist

   Ask students to develop personal checklists with homework assignments on them. Students place a square next to each subject and assignment. They insert an "x" in the appropriate square when an assignment is completed. This self-monitoring device allows students to provide reinforcement for task completion efforts. It can be used weekly.

Example:

Self Management Checklist

Name _____ Date _____

☒ Math — pp. 260-261, problems 1-20

☒ English — Grammar Book, pp. 132-134

☒ Social Studies — Project on the Gold Rush

☒ Geography — National Resources Map, Africa

☒ Spanish — p. 140, vocabulary words

☐ Human Relations — None

☐ Health — None

---

3. Time Management Program

   Conduct a unit on time management principles, including these basic time management assumptions with the group.
   Examples:

1. Use your biological clocks when planning activities. Schedule more demanding activities when your energy level is usually high.
2. When faced with difficult projects, chunk them down into pieces so they are not so overwhelming.
3. Reward yourself after each task, by a treat, phone call, exercise, or other nurturing activity.
4. Develop check lists or graphs to monitor yourself and see your progress graphically.
5. Try to set up plans to deal with problems as they occur. Avoiding them will bring on much stress.

Form task groups to investigate time management principles and apply them to members' life situations. Explore their biological clocks and determine periods of peak and low efficiency functioning. Then ask students to assist each other in designing personal time management programs.

Resource Activities*	Reference Codes	Grade Levels
1. Looking at School Controls	NM, p. 61	7-12
2. Whether or Not to Conform	NM, p. 103	9-12
3. Pins and Straws	HB V, pp. 79-84	7-12
4. Student-Student Interaction	LTA, pp. 130-135	7-12
5. Issue-Centered Writing	SCC, pp. 145-153	7-12

*See Appendix B.

152

OBJECTIVE 5

TO RESIST PEER PRESSURE AND ACT AUTONOMOUSLY

STRATEGIES

1. Portrayals of Manipulation

     Collect popular magazines and distribute them to students. Instruct the group to peruse the magazines and select pictures which show people influencing or manipulating others.

     Hold a discussion about various situations, reasons, and methods students use to change the behavior of others. Elicit students' reactions to manipulation by peers. Hold a brainstorming activity to generate alternative ways to resist others' manipulation attempts.

2. Positive and Negative Reactions

Ask students to list and describe traits they like and dislike in other people by leading a discussion on what habits, qualities, and features generate positive feelings or mobilize discomfort. Encourage the students to articulate their feelings about how certain traits might be "catching," dangerous, or offensive, and how others are seen as desirable.

Discuss how friends sometimes influence the way students act toward peers. Identify the consequences of their conformity or rebelliousness. Investigate alternative ways to handle the peer pressure to act in inappropriate ways.

3. Analysis of Cliques

Ask your group to do some field research on the nature and causes of cliques in the school setting.

Establish a one-month unit whereby students will pick a particular clique in the school and write a report including the age, gender, interests, and activities of its members. Describe the rites of membership. Invite the students to speculate on what personal needs are satisfied by the clique. Describe how the clique might affect students in the school. Be certain no students' names are mentioned in reports.

Read and discuss the papers, share information, and prepare a miniature social analysis which might become an article for the school newspaper.

4. Refusal Skills

To introduce the refusal skills to be learned and practiced, follow the seven-step procedure below:

1. Introduce the exercise with the ice breaker, **Break-in, Break-out**. Instruct the group as follows:

   Form a circle and chain of hands. One group member gets in the middle of the circle and tries to break out. Any member of the hand chain may decide to let him/her out. Or the group can band together to keep the prisoner in the middle.

   Let the action continue for three minutes. Try this technique with three or more people. This exercise is designed to illustrate coercion from group pressure. Use this as a metaphor to illustrate the effect of peer pressure on the individual. Escaping the control of others requires finesse, flexibility, and trial and error approaches. Explore the feelings and frustration produced by the power of peer bonding. Explore how it felt to escape the circle, the feelings towards the person who provided the escape route, and the aftereffects of the break-out.

154

2. Introduce **Red Flags: Situations to Avoid**. Ask the group to reassemble and brainstorm to identify typical actions and situations where saying no is a good idea. Examples are: when someone wants you to go to a dangerous neighborhood, commit a crime, harass or injure someone else. Ask one person to write the ideas down. Reproduce this list and hand it out to the group. Allow fifteen minutes for this exercise.

3. Initiate small group discussions to identify **Exit Modes**. Ask the group to form groups of four to come up with creative ways to say no to potentially harmful situations. Emphasize the fact that there are no wrong approaches, just what works. Ask the group to build a resource bank of refusal skills, write them down, and distribute them. Allow fifteen minutes.

Below are some examples of ways to exit high risk activities. They have been developed by students.

1. Invent an excuse such as, "I have other things I have to do."
2. Use delay tactics: "I'll do it tomorrow."
3. Walk away to avoid facing the situation.
4. Shift the blame and try to make the pressure group feel guilty.
5. Act ignorant about how to do something.
6. Identify the other things that are more important to do at the moment.
7. Give alternate solutions to the situation: You don't have to rip off the K-Mart to get a Walkman, you can ask your grandparent, shovel snow, do a job, etc. It is much safer.
8. Get away from the situation as soon as possible.
9. Take control of the situation. "I don't want to get high. I want to meet my girlfriend at the roller coaster now."
10. Ask them to justify why you should do what they want you to do. "What is in it for me?"

Read through all the Refusal Skills and make up an example showing how you would use each. Allow five minutes for this process. Ask the members to take turns giving examples of each technique. Direct a discussion around the leaders' reasons for using these skills, but no prolonged demonstrations should take place.

155

4.   Encourage the group to identify **Internal Resources**. Explain that we all use an array of personal resources that make it possible for us to muster up the strength to refuse to comply with coercive peer pressure to engage in potentially self-damaging activities.

To identify these states of mind in different people, divide the group into concentric circles in a "Fishbowl" motif. Ask the members of the inner circle to brainstorm their own types of inner states which "empower" them to refuse to comply with other's expectations, both positive and negative. For example, most participants know how and when to procrastinate on a task or a dangerous request. Set up roles for the outer group such as: recorder (who writes down the states), reporter of the states, and an observer of leadership roles. Then ask the outer group to add their own examples of resources.

Examples of Internal Resources and States to Say No

a) Positive attitude that validates your position.
b) Holding power to cling to your ideas.
c) Inner strength.
d) Awareness that the consequences of giving in are not worth it.
e) Sufficient hostility towards those who are trying to force you to do something against your will.
f) Confidence
g) Self-respect

Allow fifteen minutes for this exercise.

5.   Encourage the group to develop a **Symbol Check**. Ask students to think of their own special codes or symbols that they can use to remind themselves to trigger resources and attitudes that empower them to say no. The symbols might be a color, name, code, or vision that reminds them to refuse. Allow five minutes for this exercise.

6.   Set up three role-plays of typical red alert situations where a definite refusal is called for. Role-play the peer group's techniques of applying pressure, and have one or more members take turns using their symbols to get personal resources and then the actual refusal skills. Ask the group to form a consensus on which strategies work best for each situation. Allow fifteen minutes for the role-plays and discussions.

7. Do a round of sentence completion to reinforce the skills generated from the workshop. "I learned..." might be an appropriate vehicle to review the experience. Distribute refusal skill strategies to the group, and set up a phone network for further support. Encourage them to use the skills for themselves and teach them to other students.

Resource Activities*	Reference Codes	Grade Levels
1. Killer Statements and Gestures	100, pp. 67-68	7-12
2. "Rust in Peace"	NM, pp. 54-57	7-12
3. Whether or Not to Conform	NM, p. 103	9-12
4. Girls, What Do You Think You Would Do?	AB, pp. 48-49	7-12
5. Boys, What Do You Think You Would Do?	AB, pp. 50-51	7-8
6. Peer Pressure	RP, p. 43	7-8
7. Drugs	RP, p. 44	7-8
8. Dropping Out of High School	RP, p. 46	7-12
9. Ripping Off a Candy Store	RP, p. 52	7-8
10. Trouble Money	RP, pp. 254-279	7-12
11. Value Dilemmas	PE, pp. 254-279	7-12
12. Baker's Dozen	VC, pp. 383-384	7-12
13. Marijuana Story	HV, pp. 180-183	7-12
14. The Ten Commandments	DHP II, pp. 29-30	7-12
15. Needs and Responsibilities Cards	DHP II, pp. 30-31	7-12
16. War and Peace	DHP II, pp. 38-39	7-8
17. Recognizing Personal Values	D (LG), pp. 15-16 D, p. 11	9-12
18. What Do I Value?	D (LG), pp. 16-18 D, p. 12	9-12
19. Exploring Your Values	D (LG), p. 18 D, p.14	9-12
20. Using Values in Making Decisions	D (LG), p. 19 D, p.16	9-12

*See Appendix B.

157

GOAL VIII

To Develop Creativity

Through increased technology and advanced achievement, our dreams of attaining personal freedom have become both more possible and more unsettling. Despite all the scientific advancement, our society is currently faced with some troublesome technological byproducts which leave people feeling overwhelmed and full of conflict.

This section focuses on the concept of "inventiveness" as a constructive force to overcome personal inertia and status quo consciousness. It encourages students to actively seek creative solutions to complex dilemmas.

The objectives in this section run parallel and need not be addressed in a prescribed sequence. The synthesis and evaluation skills necessary to reach these objectives are at the highest levels of Bloom's (1956) Taxonomy. Many of these skills are also inherent to the objectives listed under Goal IV (Problem-Solving and Decision-Making).

The strategies incorporate problems and situations which require an alter-perspective in order to be solved. They use verbal, visual-motor, and behavioral orientations to develop inventive thought processes, promote lateral thinking, and realize novel perceptions.

It is advisable to employ warm-up strategies such as brainstorming and sensory relaxation to set the stage for creative behavior. You may also want to use guided fantasy techniques to set the mood. Ask group members to close their eyes, be silent, and be guided into an imaginary story or experience. It is surprising how vividly a journey to a mountaintop or other special place can come alive in the minds of the group members.

OBJECTIVE 1

TO DEVELOP ORIGINAL THINKING

STRATEGIES

1. Symbols of People

    Ask students to spend five minutes thinking about the outstanding characteristics of their peers. Then instruct each student to draw a picture, symbol, animal, or cartoon character that embodies the features, qualities, and attributes of one group member. Encourage spontaneity but discourage derogatory pictures. Join the process.

    After about ten minutes, invite the group to share their pictures. Ask the group to guess the person represented by each picture or symbol. Then initiate a discussion to identify the traits signified by the students' creations.

2. Group Commercial[51]

    To stimulate original thinking through group processes, ask students to form groups of five and develop their own commercials. Provide oaktag, markers, paper fasteners, scissors, and, if available, overhead projectors and wall screens. Allow two class periods for this project. Instruct the group as follows:

---

[51]This strategy was developed by Arlene Pousson, art teacher, Fort Lee Public Schools, Fort Lee, N.J. and Gary Farishian, teacher, Verona Public Schools, Verona, N.J. Used by permission of the authors.

Each group is to create and present an original commercial, based on a given theme. Cut out oaktag silhouette puppets and project them on the walls to act out your commercial.

You must work cooperatively with your group to generate as many ideas for a project theme as possible. Your group will then select the best theme on which you all agree.

The commercial must be original and clearly identify the theme your group selects. It must take from three to five minutes. All groups will present their commercials to the class and each person in the group will receive the same grade.

You should all share in decision-making, take turns talking, participate in creating the script, and share in making the puppets and actual presentation.

Your group will need a "recorder" to record ideas and the final decision the group makes, and an "observer" to watch, listen, and keep a checklist you will be given.

Use the next period to present the commercials. After all groups have shown their presentations, each group will receive feedback from the group observer. Then they will be asked to discuss the following amongst themselves:

1. What were things in your group that helped the group work well?
2. What did you do when someone in your group was not contributing?
3. What things made you feel good about your group?
4. Were there things that hindered your group's progress?
5. How could your group improve working next time?

Lead a large group discussion summarizing the process.

3. <u>Create Your Own Board Game</u>

Distribute magic markers, oaktag, a spinning dial, and small blocks to groups of four.

Set time limit of fifteen minutes and instruct groups to create their own board games. Ask the groups to design the board, the goals, and rules of the game.

Then allow students to take a test run, playing the games and refining them.

As a follow-up you might spend a period allowing different groups to trade games and play them.

4. <u>Tinker Toy Projects</u>

Divide into two groups, and ask each group to create a project with a can of Tinker Toys or box of Legos. Give five-minute time limits, enforce no-talking rule, and ask each group to name the project after five minutes. Process the experience by asking who led, who followed, why and how. Ask about changes in leadership and why people followed others. Ask about the competition between and within groups, and get reactions to the effect of time limits on performance.

Resource Activities*	Reference Codes	Grade Levels
1. Boundary Breaking Problems	DHP II, pp. 60-61	7-12
2. String and Knot	DHP II, p. 61	7-12
3. Handcuffed Together	DHP II, p. 61	7-12
4. Dime in a Bottle	DHP II, p. 62	7-12
5. The Fox, Goose, and Bag of Corn Problem	DHP II, p. 62	7-12
6. Archaeological Digs	DHP II, pp. 78-79	7-12
7. Loose Ends	CGG, pp. 21-22	7-12
8. Take A Good Look	CGG, pp. 24-25	7-12
9. Diamonds and Rubies	CGG, pp. 26-27	7-12
10. Make Something of It	CGG, pp. 34-35	9-12
11. A Woman's Ingenuity	CGG, pp. 44-45	9-12
12. Using Lateral Thinking to Solve Problems	UYO, pp. 26-28	9-12
13. Creativity Test	AE, pp. 200-202	7-12
14. Using Frustration to Stimulate Invention	GFF, pp. 168-169	7-12
15. New Twists for Old Tools	DAE, pp. 166-167	7-12
16. Broken Squares	HB I, pp. 25-29	7-12
17. Finger Collage	ICE, pp. 29-30	7-12
18. Prehistoric Animals	ICE, pp. 53-54	7-12
19. The Creature	ICE, pp. 63-64	7-12
20. Hello	ICE, pp. 301-302	7-12
21. Orchestra	TLC, p. 23	7-12
22. My Invention	TLC, p. 46	7-12

*See Appendix B.

OBJECTIVE 2

TO DEVELOP HIGHER LEVEL CONCEPTUALIZATION

STRATEGIES

1. Word Factory

   Ask the group to imagine some feelings, needs, wants, and experiences that are difficult to express in one word. Then request students to spend ten minutes creating their own words to express these personal thoughts.

   Examples of some word inventions might include:

   Wish-off: To get someone or something off your back.

   Funtastic: Supreme excitement and enjoyment.

2. Video Creations

   Ask students to imagine that they are employed by a famous video game manufacturer such as Atari or Coleco. Ask students to spend a few minutes developing a novel concept for a video game.

   Have each student provide a sketch and written description of his or her creation. Encourage the students to consider the goals, setting, objects, colors, and action flow of each game.

   Divide students into groups of four or five. Encourage them to demonstrate and embellish their games cooperatively.

   As a follow-up, have students vote to establish the group's most creative games and then forward these concepts to manufacturers.

3. Musical Odyssey

Ask students to imagine themselves as disc jockeys working in a fashionable disco. Instruct the members to search their personal music archives and design their ideal "musical set" to be woven together for dancing. Ask students to list selections on paper.

Invite the group to share their music and describe their commonalities. Then divide into groups to embellish, modify, and synthesize new "musical sets."

As a follow-up activity, ask students to bring in their record or tapes and play sample "sets."

Resource Activities*	Reference Codes	Grade Levels
1. Look What They've Done to My Brain, Ma: An Exercise in Creativity and Self-Concept	AE, pp. 203-205	7-12
2. New Games from Old	GFF, pp. 142-144	7-12
3. Asking "What Would Happen If . . .?" (I)	GFF, pp. 174-175	7-12
4. Asking "What Would Happen If . . .?" (II)	GFF, pp. 175-177	7-12
5. Futuring	DAE, pp. 160-162	7-12
6. "New Twists for Old Tools"	DAE, pp. 166-167	7-12
7. Half of Thirteen	CGG, p. 40	7-12
8. What Goes Down, But Won't Go Up?	CGG, pp. 43-44	7-12
9. Hospital's Bonanza	CGG, p. 48	9-12
10. The Greek Cross	CGG, p. 55	9-12
11. Arabs and Romans	CGG, pp. 64-65	9-12
12. Make Something of It (II)	CGG, pp. 69-70	7-12
13. Figure Completion	CGG, pp. 73-76	7-12
14. Spell It Out	CGG, p. 89	9-12
15. Many Things	CGG, pp. 93-95	9-12
16. Basket	ICE, pp. 139-140	7-12
17. Entrance Exam	ICE, pp. 131-132	9-12
18. Imagination	ICE, pp. 309-311	10-12

*See Appendix B.

APPENDICES

APPENDIX A

FEEDBACK

Name_____Group _____ Date _____

Goal No. _____ Objective No. _____ Strategy No._____

When and in what context was the strategy used (date, time of day, and type

of group)? _____

_____

Was it effective? _____ In what way(s)? _____

_____

_____

_____

Any application to other goals and objectives?

Goal No./Nos._____

_____

_____

Suggested changes: _____

_____

_____

_____

Permission to reprint: Copyright © 1990, V. Alex Kehayan, *Self-Awareness Growth Experiences*, Jalmar Press, Rolling Hills Estates, CA.

APPENDIX B

Reference Codes for Resource Activities and Addresses of Publishers and Distributors

100   — *One Hundred Ways to Enhance Self-Concept in the Classroom.* Jack Canfield and Harold Wells, 1976.

Prentice Hall, Inc.
Englewood Cliffs, N.J.
(Distributed by Jalmar Press, 45 Hitching Post Drive, Bldg. 2, Rolling Hills Estates, CA 90274)

AB   — *Dealing with Aggressive Behavior,* ESEA Title III. Educational Research Council of America, and Department of Education, Lakewood City Public Schools [Lakewood, Ohio], 1973.

Educational Research Council of America
Rockefeller Building
Cleveland, Ohio 04115

AE   — *Affective Education: Strategies for Experiential Learning.* Louis Thayer and Kent Beeler (Eds.), 1976.

University Associates
8517 Production Ave.
P.O. Box 26240
La Jolla, California 92037

AG   — *Awareness Games.* Clause Hoper, Ulrike Kutzleb, Alke Stobbe, and Bertram Weber, 1975.

St. Martins Press
175 Fifth Avenue
New York, N.Y. 10010

BVC   — *Beginning Values Clarification.* Sidney B. Simon and Jay Clark, 1975.

The Wright Group
Suite 14W
8265 Commercial Street
La Mesa, California 92401

CGG   — *Creative Growth Games.* Eugene Raudsepp and George Hough, Jr., 1980.

G.P. Putnam and Sons
200 Madison Avenue
New York, N.Y. 10016

CVSM — *Clarifying Values through Subject Matter: Application in the Classroom.* Harmin Merrill, Howard Kirschenbaum, and Sidney Simon, 1976.

Winston Press
25 Groveland Terrace
Minneapolis, Mn. 55403

D — *Deciding.* H.B. Gelatt, Barbara B. Varenhorst, and Richard Carey, 1972.

College Board Publication Orders
Box 2815
Princeton, N.J. 08540

D (LG) — *Deciding: A Leader's Guide.* H.B. Gelatt, Barbara B. Varenhorst, and Richard Carey, 1972.

College Board Publication Orders
Box 2815
Princeton, N.J. 08540

DAE — *Designs in Affective Education.* Elizabeth W. Flynn and John LaFaso, 1974.

Paulist Press
400 Sette Drive
Paramus, N.J. 07652

DHP — *Developing Human Potential.* Robert Hawley and Isabel Hawley, 1975.

ERA Press
Amherst, Mass.

DHP II — *Developing Human Potential,* Vol. II. Robert Hawley and Isabel Hawley, 1977.

ERA Press
Amherst, Mass.

DHR — *The 1985 Annual: Developing Human Resources.* Leonard D. Goodstein, and William Pfeiffer, 1985.

University Associates Inc.
8517 Production Ave.
San Diego, CA. 92121

GFF — *Giving Form to Feeling.* Nancy King, 1975.

Drama Book Specialists/Publishers
150 West 52 Street
New York, N.Y. 10019

GIT — *Getting It Together.* Beverly Mattox, 1975.

Pennant Press
Suite 14W
8265 Commercial Street
La Mesa, Cal. 92041

HB — *A Handbook of Structured Experiences.* 5 vols. William Pfeiffer and John Jones, 1971-1975.

University Associates
8517 Production Ave.
P.O. Box 26240
La Jolla, California 92037

HV — *Human Values in the Classroom.* Robert Hawley and Isabel Hawley, 1975.

A & W Publishers
95 Madison Avenue
New York, N.Y. 10010

ICE — *The Encyclopedia and Icebreakers: Structured Activities that Motivate, Challenge, Acquaint, and Energize.* Sue Forbess-Greene, 1983.

University Associates Inc.
8517 Production Ave.
San Diego, CA. 92121

LHT — *Left Handed Teaching.* Gloria Castilla, 1978.

Holt, Rinehart-Winston
383 Madison Avenue
New York, N.Y. 10017

LTA — *Learning Together and Alone.* David Johnson and Robert Johnson, 1975.

Prentice Hall, Inc.
Route 9W
Englewood Cliffs, N.J. 07632

NM — *The New Model Me. High School Student Book.* Educational Research Council of America and Lakewood Public School System [Lakewood, Ohio].

Educational Research Council of America
Rockefeller Building
Cleveland, Ohio 44115

PE — *Personalizing Education.* Leland W. Howe and Mary M. Howe, 1975.

A & W Publishers
95 Madison Avenue
New York, N.Y. 10010

RP — *Value Exploration through Role PLay.* Robert C. Hawley, 1975.

A & W Publishers
95 Madison Avenue
New York, N.Y. 10010

SCL — *Structuring Cooperative Learning: The 1980 Handbook.* Virginia M. Lyons, 1980.

Cooperative Network
University of Minneapolis
Minneapolis, Minn. 55400

TLC — *Building Interpersonal Relationships through Talking, Listening, Communicating.* Jeffrey Bormaster and Carol Treat, 1982.

Pro-Ed Publishers
5341 Industrial Oaks Blvd.
Austin, Texas 78735

UYO — *Understanding Yourself and Others.* William A. Gray and Brian A. Gerrard, 1981.

Harper and Row, Publishers
10 East 53 Street
New York, N.Y. 10022

VC — *Values Clarification: A Handbook of Practical Strategies for Teachers and Students.* Simon Sidney, Leland Howe, and Howard Kirschenbaum.

A & W Publishers
95 Madison Avenue
New York, N.Y. 10010

APPENDIX C

Addresses of Publishers and Distributors of Commercial Assessment Instruments

Behavior Rating Profile. Linda L. Brown and David D. Hammill, 1978.

> Pro-Ed Publishers
> 5341 Industrial Oaks Blvd.
> Austin, Texas 78735

Self-Esteem Inventory. Stanley Coopersmith, 1975.

> Self-Esteem Institute
> 1730 Stockton Street
> San Francisco, CA 94133

Analysis of Coping Style. G. Orville Johnson and Herbert F. Boyd, 1981.

> Charles E. Merrill Publishing Company
> Box 50S
> 1300 Alum Creek Drive
> Columbus, OH 43216

"Problem-Solving Worksheet," in *Structuring Cooperative Learning.* Virginia Lyons, 1980.

> Cooperative Learning Network
> University of Minnesota
> Minneapolis, MN 55403

Watson-Glaser Critical Thinking Appraisal. Goodwin Watson and Edwin M. Glaser, 1980.

> Psychological Corporation
> 757 Third Avenue
> New York, NY 10017

The Personality Inventory for Children. Robert D. Wirl, David Lackar, James E. Klinedinst, Philip D. Scot, and William E. Broen, Jr., 1979.

> Western Psychological Services
> 12031 Wilshire Blvd.
> Los Angeles, CA 90025

APPENDIX D

Additional Strategy Applications

GOAL I: TO INCREASE SELF-AWARENESS

Objective 1: To discover feelings and needs

Strategies

Objective 2: To demonstrate understanding of feelings by describing situations which arouse such emotions as fear, anger, or joy

Strategies

Objective 3: To communicate feelings, ideas and needs effectively

Strategies

GOAL II: TO DEVELOP SELF-ESTEEM

Objective 1: To refrain from self-devaluation

Strategies

Objective 2: To develop awareness of positive qualities and skills

Strategies

Objective 3: To adapt to new situations and join new activities

Strategies

Objective 4: To develop a repertoire of appropriate assertive responses

Strategies

GOAL III: TO IMPROVE SOCIAL INTERACTION SKILLS

Objective 1: To relate positively to new people

Strategies

Objective 2: To participate in discussions and activities with peers

Strategies

Objective 3: To act supportively toward others

<u>Strategies</u>

177

Objective 6: To sustain friendships with peers

Strategies

Objective 7: To respond positively to teachers and other authority figures

Strategies

GOAL IV: TO DEVELOP PROBLEM-SOLVING AND DECISION-MAKING SKILLS

Objective 1: To recognize when a conflict situation exists in stories, hypothetical cases or role-playing activities

179

Objective 4: To express preferences in personal choices and goals

Strategies

Objective 2: To complete assignments thoroughly within given time limits

Strategies

Objective 3: To recognize realistic abilities and limitations

Strategies

Objective 4: To respond appropriately to hostility and criticism from others

Strategies

Objective 5: To deal with school's discipline requirements

Strategies

Objective 6: To use inner controls to promote responses other than impulsive behavior

Strategies

Objective 7: To cope with stress and frustrating experiences

Strategies

184

GOAL VII: TO DEVELOP INDEPENDENT FUNCTIONING

Objective 1: To follow directions without individual assistance

Strategies

Objective 2: To approach learning tasks in an organized, non-impulsive manner

Strategies

Objective 3: To use leisure time productively

Strategies

Objective 4: To develop self-monitoring skills

Strategies

Objective 5: To resist peer pressure and act autonomously

Strategies

GOAL VIII: TO DEVELOP CREATIVITY

Objective 1: To develop original thinking

Strategies

**Objective 2: To develop higher level
conceptualization**

Strategies

APPENDIX E

A Brief Historical Background of
Personal Growth Education

The current personal growth educational trend employs a collection of approaches evolving from the Human Potential Movement, which began in the late 1950s and early 1960s. This movement's philosophy is based on the assumption that human beings can take responsibility to attain personal satisfaction. Humanistic approaches to education throughout the 1960s and 1970s saw many paradoxes and conflicts reflected by the contradictory goals imposed by the society at large. Dichotomies inherent to the educational mission, such as conformity versus self-fulfillment, competition versus collaboration, responsibility versus freedom, and independence versus interdependence, created a series of diverse approaches to personal growth education. The goals, objectives, and interventions presented in *SAGE* attempt to incorporate both sides of these dichotomies. They embody an amalgam of ideas and principles promoted by the pioneers of the Human Potential Movement.

Some of the earliest groundwork for personal growth education was laid by John Dewey, Maria Montessori, Jerome Bruner, and John Piaget. These pioneers advocated experiential learning as a vehicle to attain personal growth, freedom, and responsibility to self and others. Fortunately, learning by doing has continued to flourish in our schools.

The 1970s witnessed an explosion of personal growth, educational techniques designed to promote self-actualization, a concept spawned by Abraham Maslow (1954). Maslow developed a Needs Hierarchy which began with the satisfaction of physiological needs such as food. The human growth process progressed through the satisfaction of safety, security, and belongingness needs which culminated with the attainment of love and respect. Maslow stated that human beings progress through these stages in a quest to attain the altruistic, energetic, and creative state of self-actualization. Maslow's humanistic ideals of self-direction, openness, and collaboration were supported by such pioneers as Carl Rogers, Haiam Ginott, Erik Erikson, and Rollo May, all of whom believed in a spirit of inquiry, free will, and self-discovery.

Personal growth education also adopted its approaches from Gestalt Psychology, which emphasized the effect of human perception upon learning, growth, and social interactions. Human polarities, such as love/hate, feeling/thinking, self-fulfillment/self-destruction, inherent in Jung's (1954) philosophy of human development were embellished by Fritz Perls, who became the major spokesman for the Gestalt movement. Perls (1967) developed a variety of techniques which enabled people to discover and to confront their dark sides. His approach helped people to assume responsibility for their own behavior and become integrated, well functioning human beings.

The Encounter Group Movement produced an array of growth centers such as the National Training Laboratories, the Esalen Institute, the Erhard Seminars Training (EST). These centers sprang up during the past two decades. Contemporary advances in the movement have been introduced into the field of education by such authors as Geroge Brown (*Confluent Education*, 1971), Thomas Harris (*Transactional Analysis*, 1967), and Thomas Gordon (*Teacher Effectiveness Training*, 1974).

The Behaviorist School of Psychology is an approach to human development which ran parallel to the humanistic orientation. Ivan Pavlov and John Watson founded the Behaviorist School. B. F. Skinner, Albert Bandura, Donald Miechenbaum, and others have extended this work and applied it to education. Unlike the Humanistic School, the Behaviorists attribute most behavior to external agents. The so-called inner forces, drives, self-perceptions, and free will are rendered unobservable and difficult to measure. Instead, the Behaviorists attempt to change behavior through external reinforcers and non-reinforcers. The Behaviorist School points out the difficulties in defining and measuring such vague concepts as positive self-esteem, self-disclosure, and personal needs.

Because our learning institutions reflect society's values and expectations, techniques such as behavior modification and behavior management have found their place in American education. The Management by Objectives Movement and the new legislation governing the education of the handicapped have employed clearly designated goals with interventions designed to attain them. Frequent evaluation and assessment techniques have been applied to the behavior-change guidelines in our schools.

Albert Bandura (1967) provided a set of guiding principles which greatly influenced our educational technology. Using Modeling Theory, he developed new methods to enable students to learn by observing the behavior of others and then by incorporating new patterns into what he termed self-monitoring systems. Peer-assistance systems, group process learning, role-playing techniques, and fading procedures (Miechenbaum, 1977) have promoted more acceptable behavior patterns in students.

A recent approach to promote personal growth in schools is Values Clarification. Pioneered by Sidney Simon, Leland Howe, and Howard Kirshenbaum (1972), Values Clarification enables students to examine their lives, values, and personal priorities. The technique avoids values inculcation; instead it seeks to enhance self-discovery through structured, experiential exercises. Values Clarification uses non-judgmental vehicles to promote personal growth.

Values Clarification often leads to the exploration of moral and ethical issues. Lawrence Kohlberg, a pioneer in this area, formulated a set of principles that stressed moral development. Kohlberg's orientation sought to foster a higher sense of ethics in our children. Working with colleagues at Harvard University, Kohlberg established a hierarchy of six growth patterns grouped into three levels: Pre-Conventional, Conventional, and Post-Conventional (Kohlberg, Turiel & Lesser, 1971). According to Kohlberg, an individual moves from behavior motivated by intrinsic needs to behavior motivated by altruistic and universal principles. Few individuals ever reach the highest ethical levels at Stage 3 (Kohlberg, 1973).

Beverly Mattox and her associates (1975) developed a series of role-playing activities to foster the exploration of morality among our nation's students. These techniques have found a place in the affective curricula in many of our schools.

Recent legislation in many states has produced a revival of educational approaches tailored to the gifted and talented. These approaches focus on promotion of imagination and original thinking. A multitude of worthwhile techniques designed to teach creativity has grown out of the gifted and talented orientation. Pioneers in this field, such as Alex Osborn, Donald MacKinnon, and Frank Baron, laid the foundation for new approaches to promote enrichment programs intended to enhance the right-brain functions of visual and intuitive learning.

Our society's increased complexity, with its attendant anxiety-producing situations, requires that maturing students develop skills to sharpen their perceptions and original thinking. Authors such as Eugene Raudsepp and George Hough, Jr. (1980), and Doris Shallcross (1981) have developed new techniques to enhance the creative processes in our students.

Along the same lines, the infusion of Eastern philosophies over the past two decades has served to introduce sensory awareness techniques into the schools as vehicles which allow students to acquire an altered perception of life's dilemmas. Students are taught to experience their stress points in various parts of their bodies. They learn how to transfer the stress through and out of their bodies and to dissipate their pain and tension through self-induced stress-management techniques. Movement and space activities also teach children to become more physically and mentally grounded and capable of coping with life's stresses realistically.

Another recent trend, Family Life Education, has also found its place in our schools. Families in many states have influenced their local schools to develop new types of curricula in this area. Programs have emerged to promote students' development of responsible behavior and social consciousness. This new emphasis has placed responsibilities on boards of education to address the impact on our youth of sexual values, family roles, sibling relationships, substance abuse, and religion. The approaches marshaled by these Family Life Programs adopt many of the principles promoted by the Humanistic Education Movement.

Despite the seemingly disparate elements of these theoretical perspectives, they all seem to share a common emphasis on interpersonal relationships, social survival, and harmony. Some of the frameworks mentioned above have been labeled controversial by various groups who have taken issue with their legitimacy or appropriateness. Yet, despite the criticism, the emphasis on personal-social development maintains a vital position in the public domain. The movement continues to grow and evolve to meet the current needs of our society's young people.

The goals, objectives, and approaches described in *SAGE* are derived from the theories mentioned above. Many of them overlap; yet all of them have been designed to meet the challenge of current issues in personalized education.

REFERENCES

Adler, Gerhart, et al. (Eds.). *The Collected Works of Carl G. Jung.* Trans. R.F. Hull. Princeton, N.J.: Princeton University Press, 1954. Rev. ed., 1971.

Bandura, Albert. "Behavioral Psychotherapy." *Scientific America*, Vol. 216, No. 3 (March 1967), pp. 78-86.

Barron, Frank. *Creative Person and Creative Process.* New York: Holt, Rinehart and Winston, 1969.

Bern, Eric. *Transactional Analysis in Psychotherapy.* New York: Grove Press, 1961.

Bloom, Benjamin S. (Ed.). *Taxonomy of Educational Objectives: The Classification of Educational Goals by a Committee of College and University Examiners.* New York: Longmans, Green, 1956.

Bormaster, Jeffrey, and Treat, Carol. *Building Interpersonal Relationships through Talking Listening, Communicating.* Austin, Texas: Pro-Ed 1982.

Brown, George I. *Human Teaching for Human Learning.* San Francisco: Esalen Institute, 1971.

Brown, Linda L., and Hammill, Donald D. *Behavior Rating Profile.* Austin, Texas: Pro-Ed Publishers, 1978.

Canfield, Jack, and Wells, Harold. *One Hundred Ways to Enhance Self-Concept in the Classroom.* Englewood Cliffs, N.J.: Prentice Hall, 1976.

Castillo, Gloria. *Left Handed Teaching.* 2nd ed. New York: Holt, Rinehart and Winston, 1978.

Cleaveland B. *Mastering Teaching Techniques.* Muskego, WI.; The Connecting Link Press, 1986.

Educational Research Council of America, and Department of Education, Lakewood City Public Schools [Lakewood, Ohio]. *Dealing with Aggressive Behavior.* ESEA Title III. Cleveland: Educational Research Council of America, 1973.

_____, and Lakewood Public School System [Lakewood, Ohio]. *The New Model Me. High School Student Book.* Cleveland: Educational Research Council of America, 1973.

Erikson, Erik. *Childhood and Society*. New York: W.W. Norton and Company, 1963.

Flynn, Elizabeth W., and LaFaso, John. *Designs in Affective Education*. New York: Paulist Press, 1974.

Gelatt, H.B., Varenhorst, Barbara T., and Carey, Richard. *Deciding*. New York: College Entrance Examination Board, 1972.

_____, Varenhorst, Barbara T., and Carey, Richard. *Deciding: A Leader's Guide*. New York: College Entrance Examination Board, 1972.

Ginott, Haim. *Teacher and Child*. New York: Macmillan, 1972.

Goodstein, Leonard and Pfeiffer, J. William. *The 1985 Annual: Developing Human Resources*. San Diego: University Associates, 1983.

Gordon, Thomas. *Teacher Effectiveness Training*. New York: Peter H. Wyden, 1974.

Gray, William A., and Gerrard, Brian A. *Understanding Yourself and Others*. New York: Harper and Row, 1981.

Greene, Sue Forbess. *The Encyclopedia and Icebreakers: Structured Activities that Motivate, Challenge, Acquaint, and Energize*. San Diego: University Associates, 1985.

Harmin, Merrill, Kirschenbaum, Howard, and Simon, Sidney. *Clarifying Values through Subject Matter: Application in the Classroom*. Minneapolis: Winston Press, Inc., 1976.

Harris, Thomas A. *I'm O.K., You're O.K.* New York: Harper and Row, 1967.

Hawley, Robert. *Value Exploration through Role Playing*. New York: Hart Publishing Co., 1975.

_____, and Hawley, Isabel. *Developing Human Potential*. Amherst, Mass.: Education Research Associates, 1975.

_____, and Hawley, Isabel. *Developing Human Potential*. Vol. II. Amherst, Mass.: Education Research Associates, 1977.

_____, and Hawley, Isabel. *Human Values in the Classroom*. New York: Hart Publishing Co., 1975.

Hawley, Robert C., and Hawley, Isabel L. "Scissors, Glue and English, Too." *Independent School Bulletin*, Vol. 33, No. 1 (October 1973), pp. 41-43.

Höper, Clause, Kutzleb, Ulrike, Stobbe, Alke, and Weber, Bertram. *Awareness Games.* New York: St. Martins Press, 1975.

Howe, Leland W., and Howe, Mary M. *Personalizing Education.* New York: Hart Publishing Company, 1975.

Johnson, David W., and Johnson, Robert T. *Learning Together and Alone.* Englewood Cliffs, N.J.: Prentice Hall, Inc., 1975.

Johnson, G. Orville, and Boyd, Hubert F. *Analysis of Coping Style.* Columbus, Ohio: Charles E. Merrill Publishing Co., 1981.

Jung, Carl G. *Analytical Psychology: Its Theory and Practice. The Tavistock Lectures, 1935.* New York: Pantheon Books, 1968.

King, Nancy. *Giving Form to Feeling.* New York: Drama Books Specialists/Publishers, 1975.

Kohlberg, Lawrence, "Collected Papers on Moral Development and Moral Education." Cambridge: Harvard University Laboratory of Human Development, 1973. (Mimeographed.)

_____, and Turiel, Edward. "Moral Development and Moral Education." In G. Lesser (Ed.). *Psychology and the Educational Process.* Chicago: Scott, Foresman, 1971.

Lyons, Virginia M. *Structuring Cooperative Learning. The 1980 Handbook.* Minneapolis: Cooperation Network Publications, 1980.

MacKinnon, Donald W. *In Search of Human Effectiveness: Identifying and Developing Creativity.* Buffalo, N.Y.: Creative Education Foundation: Great Neck, N.Y.: Creative Synergetic Associates, 1978.

Maslow, Abraham. *Motivation and Personality.* New York: Harper and Row, 1954.

Mattox, Beverly. *Getting It Together.* La Mesa, Cal.: Pennant Press, 1975.

May, Rollo. *Love and Will.* New York: Random House, 1968.

Meichenbaum, Donald, and Goodman, Joseph. "Training Impulsive Children to Talk to Themselves: A Means of Developing Self-Control." *Journal of Abnormal Psychology*, Vol. 77, No. 2 (April 1971), pp. 115-126.

Osborn, Alex F. *Applied Imagination.* 3rd rev. ed. New York: Charles Scribner's and Sons, 1963.

Pavlov, Ivan P. *Conditioned Reflexes.* Trans. and ed. by G.V. Anrep. New York: Dover Publications, 1960.

Perls, Fritz. *Gestalt Therapy Verbatim.* Moab, Utah: Real People Press, 1967.

Pfeiffer, William, and Jones, John. *A Handbook of Structured Experiences for Human Relations.* 5 vols. La Jolla, Cal.: University Associates, 1971-1975.

Raudsepp, Eugene, and Pough, George, Jr. *Creative Growth Games.* New York: G.P. Putnam's Sons, 1980.

Rogers, Carl R. *Freedom to Learn.* Columbus, Ohio: Merrill, 1969.

Shallcross, Doris J. *Teaching Creative Behavior.* Englewood Cliffs, N.J.: Prentice Hall, Inc., 1981.

Simon, Sidney B., and Clark, Jay. *Beginning Values Clarification.* La Mesa, Cal.: Pennant Press, 1975.

_____, Howe, Leland, and Kirschenbaum, Howard. *Values Clarification: A Handbook of Practical Strategies for Teachers and Students.* New York: Hart Publishing Company, 1972.

Skinner, B.F. *Beyond Freedom and Dignity.* New York: A.A. Knopf, 1971.

Tancil, Sallie E. "Force Field Analysis." *NEA Journal*, Vol. 57, No. 3 (March 1968), pp. 22-23.

Thayer, Louis, and Beeler, Kent (Eds.). *Affective Education Strategies for Experiential Learning.* La Jolla, Cal.: University Associates, 1976.

Watson, Goodwin, and Glaser, Edwin M. *Watson-Glaser Critical Thinking Appraisal.* New York: Psychological Corporation, 1980.

Watson, John B., and Rayner, Rosalie. "Conditioned Emotional Reactions." *Journal of Experimental Psychology*, Vol. 3 (1920), pp. 1-14.

Wirl, Robert D., Lackar, David, Klinedinst, James E., Scot, Philip D., and Broen, William E., Jr. *The Personality Inventory for Children.* Los Angeles: Western Psychological Services, 1979.

Wolpe, John, and Lazarus, Arnold. *Behavior Therapy Techniques: A Guide to the Treatment of Neuroses.* Oxford: Pergamon Press, 1966.

EXTEND THE ACTIVITIES OF *SAGE*

Unlocking Doors to Self-Esteem
by C. Lynn Fox, Ph.D. and Francine Weaver, M.A.
Jalmar Press
Grades: 7-12

A valuable resource for teachers who want to foster more loving, caring, and cooperative relationships among their students. Over 100 lesson plans and activities are included and have been designed for easy infusion into English, Drama and Communication, Social Science, Science, Career and PE classes. The format is simple, clear, and easy-to-use and an extensive resource list is included. Key concepts covered are:

• Developing Positive Self-Concepts
• Examining One's Own Attitudes, Feelings, and Actions
• Fostering Positive Relationships with Others.

"All educational settings and universities should consider this work for purchase."
—Voice of Youth Advocates

TA for Teens
by Alvyn M. Freed
Jalmar Press
Grades: 7-12

The teen years don't have to be difficult if young people understand their own feelings and the feelings of others. TA FOR TEENS presents guidelines that help teenagers cope with and understand their problems. Dr. Freed uses the concept of Transactional Analysis to explain the ups and downs of young adulthood. Without talking down to teens, TA FOR TEENS deals frankly with the topics of drugs, sex, authority, rebellion and independence. An excellent counseling tool, this book has been used in schools, youth groups, churches, and homes.

TA for Kids (and grownups, too)
by Alvyn M. Freed
Jalmar Press
Grades: 4-8

The message of Transactional Analysis is presented in simple, clear terms so students can apply it in their daily lives. Warm Fuzzies and Cold Pricklies make the concepts of social interation fun and easy to understand. TA FOR KIDS helps establish behavior patterns at school and at home...helps develop confidence and a feeling of self worth. Delightful illustrations, common sense, and humor make this book an effective social development tool.

Reading, Writing, and Rage
by Dorothy Fink Ungerleider, M.A.
Foreword by Bruce Jenner
Jalmar Press
All Grades

An autopsy of one profound school failure, disclosing the complex processes behind it and the secret rage that grew out of it. Must reading for anyone working with learning disabled, functional illiterates, or juvenile delinquents.

"The descriptive is crisp, angry and effective, and is also infuriating and familiar. I'm convinced this book will be important."
—Jonathan Kozol
The Literate America

"...a sensitive, moving story that both educates and stirs up feelings...this book might do more to force public school professionals to rethink their responsibilities toward learning disabled children than any previous publication."
—Larry B. Silver, M.D.
National Institute of Mental Health

The Turbulent Teens
Understanding, Helping, Surviving
by James Gardner, Ph.D.
Jalmar Press
Grades: 7-12

This book will help you deal successfully with the endless variety of crises associated with the teen years. Here is the insight and encouragement needed to improve the adult's ability to influence and assist the often troubled and troublesome youngsters. With directness and practicality, the book confronts sex, drugs, the generation gap, the meaning of work, the value of money, and the effectiveness of quality parenting.

20 YEARS
AWARD WINNING PUBLISHER

Order NOW 10% Discount On 3 Or More Titles!

At Last . . . You Can Be That
"MOST MEMORABLE" PARENT/TEACHER/CARE-GIVER
To Every Person Whose Life You Touch Including Yours!

HELP KIDS TO: ❖ IMPROVE GRADES   ❖ INCREASE CLASS PARTICIPATION   ❖ BECOME MORE ATTENTIVE
ENCOURAGE & INSPIRE THEM AND YOU TO: ❖ TACKLE PROBLEMS   ❖ ACHIEVE GOALS
AND
IMPROVE SELF-ESTEEM — BOTH THEIRS AND YOURS

Our authors are not just writers, but researchers and practitioners. Our books are not just written, but proven effective. All 100% tested, 100% practical, 100% effective. Look over our titles, choose the ones you want, and send your order today. You'll be glad you did. Just remember, our books are "SIMPLY THE BEST."   *Bradley L. Winch, Ph.D., JD — President and Publisher*

Project Self-Esteem, Expanded (Gr. K-8)

Innovative *parent involvement program.* Used by over 2000 schools/400,000 participants. Teaches children to respect themselves and others, make sound decisions, honor personal and family value systems, develop vocabulary, attitude, goals and behavior needed for *successful living,* practice *responsible behavior* and *avoid drug and alcohol use.*

Sandy Mc Daniel & Peggy Bielen

0-915190-59-1, 112 pages, **JP-9059-1 $39.95**
8½ x 11, paperback, illus., reprod. act. sheets

Esteem Builders (Gr. K-8)

Teach self-esteem via curriculum content. Best K-8 program available. Uses 5 building blocks of self-esteem (security/selfhood/affiliation/mission/competence) as base. Over 250 grade level/curric. content cross-correlated activities. Also assess. tool, checklist of educator behaviors for modeling, 40 week lesson planner, ext. bibliography and more.

Paperback, 64 pages, **JP-9053-2 $39.95**
Spiral bound, **JP-9088-5 $44.95**, 8½ x 11, illus.

Michele Borba, Ph.D.

NOT JUST AUTHORS BUT RESEARCHERS AND PRACTITIONERS.

Learning The Skills of Peacemaking: Communicating/Cooperation/Resolving Conflict (Gr. K-8)

Help kids say "No" to fighting. Establish WIN/WIN guidelines for conflicts in your classroom. *Over fifty lessons:* peace begins with me; integrating peacemaking into our lives; exploring our roots and inter-connectedness. Great for *self-esteem* and *cultural diversity* programs.

Naomi Drew, M.A.

0-915190-46-X, 112 pages, **JP-9046-X $21.95**
8½ x 11, paperback, illus., reprod. act. sheets

6 Vital Ingredients of Self-Esteem: How To Develop Them In Your Students (Gr. K-12)

Put self-esteem to work for your students. Learn practical ways to help kids manage school, make decisions, accept consequences, make time, and discipline themselves to set worthwhile goals...and much more. Covers developmental stages from ages 2 to 18, with implications for self-esteem at each stage.

0-915190-72-9, 192 pages, **JP-9072-9 $19.95**
8½ x 11, paperback, biblio., appendices

Bettie B. Youngs, Ph.D.

NOT JUST WRITTEN BUT PROVEN EFFECTIVE.

You & Self-Esteem: The Key To Happiness & Success (Gr. 5-12)

Comprehensive *workbook* for young people. Defines self-esteem and its importance in their lives; helps them identify why and how it adds or detracts from their vitality; shows them how to protect it from being shattered by others; outlines a plan of action to keep their self-esteem positive. Very useful.

Bettie B. Youngs, Ph.D.

0-915190-83-4, 128 pages, **JP-9083-4 $14.95**
8½ x 11, paperback, biblio., appendices

Partners for Change: Peer Helping Guide For Training and Prevention (Gr. K-12)

This comprehensive program guide provides an excellent *peer support program* for program coordinators, peer leaders, professionals, group homes, churches, social agencies, and schools. *Covers 12 areas,* including suicide, HIV / Aids, child abuse, teen pregnancy, substance abuse, low self esteem, dropouts, child abduction. etc.

Paperback, 464 pages, **JP-9069-9 $44.95**
Spiral bound, **JP-9087-7 $49.95**, 8½ x 11, illus.

V. Alex Kehayan, Ed.D.

100% TESTED — 100% PRACTICAL — 100% GUARANTEED.

Self-Awareness Growth Experiences (Gr. 7-12)

Over *593 strategies*/activities covering affective learning goals and objectives. To increase: self-awareness/self-esteem/social inter-action skills/problem-solving, decision-making skills/coping ability/ethical standards/independent functioning/creativity. Great *secondary resource.* Useful in counseling situations.

V. Alex Kehayan, Ed.D.

0-915190-61-3, 224 pages, **JP-9061-3 $16.95**
6 x 9, paperback, illus., 593 activities

Unlocking Doors to Self-Esteem (Gr. 7-12)

Contains *curriculum content objectives* with *underlying social objectives.* Teach both at the same time. Content objectives in English/Drama/Social Science/Career Education/Science/Physical Education/Social objectives in Developing Positive Self-Concepts/Examining Attitudes, Feelings and Actions/Fostering Positive Relationships.

0-915190-60-5, 224 pages, **JP-9060-5 $16.95**
6 x 9, paperback, illus., 100 lesson plans

C. Lynn Fox, Ph.D. & Francine L. Weaver, M.A.

ORDER FROM: B.L. Winch & Associates/Jalmar Press, 45 Hitching Post Drive, Bldg. 2, Rolling Hills Estates, CA 90274-5169
CALL TOLL FREE — (800) 662-9662. • (310) 547-1240 • FAX (310) 547-1644 • Add 10% shipping; $3 minimum   4/92

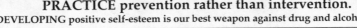

PRACTICE prevention rather than intervention.
DEVELOPING positive self-esteem is our best weapon against drug and alcohol abuse.

20 YEAR AWARD WINNING PUBLISHER

Order NOW 10% Discount On 3 Or More Titles!

Good Morning Class - I Love You (Staff)

Contains thought provoking quotes and ques-tions about teaching from the heart. Helps love become an integral part of the learning that goes on in every classroom. Great for new teachers and for experienced teachers who sometimes become frustrated by the system. Use this book to begin and end your day. Greet your students every day with: "Good morning class - I love you."

Esther Wright, M.A.

0-915190-58-3, 80 pages, **JP-9058-3 $7.95**
5½ x 8½, paperback, illus./**Button $1.50**

Enhancing Educator's Self-Esteem: It's Criterion #1 (K-12/Staff)

For the educator, a healthy self-esteem is job criteria No. 1! When high, it empowers us and adds to the vitality of our lives; when low it saps energy, erodes our confidence, lowers productivity and blocks our initiative to care about self and others. Follow the plan of action in this great resource to develop your self-esteem.

0-915190-79-6, 144 pages, **JP-9079-6 $16.95**
8½ x 11, paperback

Bettie B. Youngs, Ph.D.

NOT JUST AUTHORS BUT RESEARCHERS AND PRACTITIONERS.

I Am a Blade of Grass (Staff)

Create a school where all — students, teachers, administrators, and parents — see themselves as both learners and leaders in partnership. Develop a new compact for learning that focuses on results, that promotes local initiative and that empowers people at all levels of the system. How to in this collaborative curriculum. Great for self-esteem.

Elaine Young, M.A.
with R. Frelow, Ph.D.

0-915190-54-0, 176 pages, **JP-9054-0 $14.95**
6 x 9, paperback, illustrations

Stress Management for Educators: A Guide to Manage Our Response to Stress (Staff)

Answers these significant questions for educators: What is stress? What causes it? How do I cope with it? What can be done to manage stress to moderate its negative effects? Can stress be used to advantage? How can educators be stress-proofed to help them remain at peak performance? How do I keep going in spite of it?

0-915190-77-X, 112 pages, **JP-9077-X $12.95**
8½ x 11, paperback, illus., charts

Bettie B. Youngs, Ph.D.

NOT JUST WRITTEN BUT PROVEN EFFECTIVE.

He Hit Me Back First: Self-Esteem Through Self-Discipline (Gr. K-8)

By whose authority does a child choose right from wrong? Here are activities directed toward developing within the child an awareness of his own inner authority and ability to choose (will power) and the resulting sense of responsibility, freedom and self-esteem. 29 seperate activities.

Eva D. Fugitt, M.A.

0-915190-64-8, 120 pages, **JP-9064-8 $12.95**
8½ x 11, paperback, appendix, biblio.

Self-Esteem: The "Affiliation" Building Block (Gr. K-6)

Making friends is easy with the activities in this thoroughly researched book. Students are paired, get to know about each other, produce a book about their new friend, and present it in class. Exciting activities help discover commonalities. Great *self-esteem booster.* Revised after 10 years of field testing. Over 18 activities.

0-915190-75-3, 192 pages, **JP-9075-3 $19.95**
8½ x 11, paperback, illustrations, activities

C. Lynn Fox, Ph.D.

100% TESTED — 100% PRACTICAL — 100% GUARANTEED.

Feel Better Now: 30 Ways to Handle Frustration in Three Minutes or Less (Staff/Personal)

Teaches people to handle stress *as it happens* rapidly and directly. This basic require-ment for emotional survival and physical health can be learned with the methods in this book. Find your own recipe for relief. Foreword by Ken Keyes, Jr. "*A mine of practical help*" — says Rev. Robert Schuller.

Chris Schriner, Rel.D.

0-915190-66-4, 180 pages, **JP-9066-4 $9.95**
6 x 9, paperback, appendix, bibliography

Peace in 100 Languages: A One-Word Multilingual Dictionary (Staff Personal)

A candidate for the Guinness Book of World Records, it is the *largest/smallest dictionary ever published.* Envisioned, researched and developed by new Russian peace activists. Ancient, national, local and special languages covered. A portion of purchase price will be donated to joint U.S./Russian peace project.

0-915190-74-5, 48 pages, **JP-9074-5 $9.95**
5 x 10, glossy paperback, full color

By M. Kabattchenko,
V. Kochurov,
L. Koshanova,
E. Kononenko,
D. Kuznetsov,
A. Lapitsky,
V. Monakov,
L. Stoupin, and
A. Zagorsky

ORDER NOW FOR 10% DISCOUNT ON 3 OR MORE TITLES.

Learning to Live, Learning to Love (Staff/Personal)

Important things are often quite simple. But simple things are not necessarily easy. If you are finding that learning to live and learning to love are at times difficult, you are in good company. People everywhere are finding it a tough challenge. This simple book will help. *Shows how to separate "treasure" from "trash" in our lives.*

Joanne Haynes-Klassen

0-915190-38-9, 160 pages, **JP-9038-9 $7.95**
6 x 9, paperback, illustrations

Reading, Writing and Rage (Staff)

An autopsy of one profound *school failure,* disclosing the complex processes behind it and the *secret rage* that grew out of it. Developed from educational therapist's viewpoint. A must reading for anyone working with the *learning disabled, functional illiterates* or *juvenile delinquents.* Reads like fiction. Foreword by Bruce Jenner.

0-915190-42-7, 240 pages, **JP-9042-7 $16.95**
5½ x 8½, paperback, biblio., resources

D. Ungerleider, M.A.

ORDER FROM: B.L. Winch & Associates/Jalmar Press, 45 Hitching Post Drive, Bldg. 2, Rolling Hills Estates, CA 90274-5169
CALL TOLL FREE — (800) 662-9662. • (310) 547-1240. • FAX (310) 547-1644 • Add 10% shipping; $3 minimum   4/92

20 YEARS
AWARD WINNING
PUBLISHER

DISCOVER books on self-esteem for kids.
ENJOY great reading with Warm Fuzzies and Squib, the adventurous owl.

Larry Shles, M.A.

Moths & Mothers/Feathers & Fathers: The Story of Squib, The Owl, Begins (Ages 5-105)

Heartwarming story of a tiny owl who cannot fly or hoot as he learns to put words with his feelings. He faces frustration, grief, fear, guilt and loneliness in his life, just as we do. Struggling with these *feelings*, he searches, at least, for *understanding*. *Delightfully illustrated*. Ageless.

0-915190-57-5, 72 pages, **JP-9057-5** **$7.95**
8½ x 11, paperback, illustrations

Hoots & Toots & Hairy Brutes: The Continuing Adventures of Squib, The Owl (Ages 5-105)

Squib, who can only toot, sets out to learn how to give a mighty hoot. Even the *owl-odontist* can't help and he fails completely. Every reader who has struggled with *life's limitations* will recognize his own struggles and triumphs in the microcosm of Squib's forest world. A parable for all ages.

0-915190-56-7, 72 pages, **JP-9056-7** **$7.95**
8½ x 11, paperback, illustrations

Larry Shles, M.A.

NOT JUST AUTHORS BUT RESEARCHERS AND PRACTITIONERS.

Larry Shles, M.A.

Hugs & Shrugs: The Continuing Saga of Squib, The Owl (Ages 5-105)

Squib feels lonely, depressed and incomplete. His reflection in the pond shows that he has lost a piece of himself. He thinks his missing piece fell out and he searches in vain outside of himself to find it. Only when he discovers that it fell in and not out does he find *inner-peace* and become whole. Delightfully illustrated. Ageless.

0-915190-47-8, 72 pages, **JP-9047-8** **$7.95**
8½ x 11, paperback, illustrations

Aliens in my Nest: Squib Meets the Teen Creature (Ages 5-105)

What does it feel like to face a snarly, surly, defiant and non-communicative older brother turned *adolescent*? Friends, dress code, temperament, entertainment, room decor, eating habits, authority, music, isolation, *internal and external conflict* and many other areas of change are dealt with. Explores how to handle every situation.

0-915190-49-4, 80 pages, **JP-9049-4** **$7.95**
8½ x 11, paperback, illustrations

Larry Shles, M.A.

NOT JUST WRITTEN BUT PROVEN EFFECTIVE.

Larry Shles, M.A.

Do I Have to Go to School Today? Squib Measures Up! (Ages 5-105)

Squib dreads going to school. He daydreams about all the reasons he has not to go: the school bus will swallow him, the older kids will be mean to him, numbers and letters confuse him, he is too small for sports, etc. But, in the end, he goes because his *teacher accepts him "just as he is."* Very esteeming. Great metaphor for all ages.

0-915190-62-1, 64 pages, **JP-9062-1** **$7.95**
8½ x 11, paperback, illustrations

**Scooter's Tail of Terror
A Fable of Addiction and Hope (Ages 5-105)**

Well-known author and illustrator, Larry Shles, introduces a new forest character — a squirrel named Scooter. He faces the challenge of addiction, but is offered a way to overcome it. As with the Squib books, the story is *simple*, yet the message is *dramatic*. The story touches the child within each reader and *presents the realities of addiction*.

0-915190-89-3, 80 pages, **JP-9089-3** **$9.95**
8½ x 11, paperback, illustrations

NEW

Larry Shles, M.A.

100% TESTED — 100% PRACTICAL — 100% GUARANTEED.

REVISED

Alvyn Freed, Ph.D.

TA for Tots (and other prinzes) Revised (Gr. PreK-3)

Over 500,000 sold. New upright format. Book has helped thousands of young children and their parents to better understand and relate to each other. Helps youngsters realize their *intrinsic worth* as human beings; builds and strengthens their *self-esteem. Simple* to understand. **Coloring Book $1.95 / I'm OK Poster $3**

0-915190-73-7, 144 pages, **JP-9073-7** **$14.95**
8½ x 11, paperback, delightful illustrations

TA for Kids (and grown-ups too) (Gr. 4-9)

Over 250,000 sold. An ideal book to help youngsters develop *self-esteem,* esteem of others, *personal and social responsibility,* critical thinking and independent judgment. Book recognizes that each person is a unique human being with the capacity to learn, grow and develop. Hurray for TA! Great for parents and other care givers.

0-915190-09-5, 112 pages, **JP-9009-5** **$9.95**
8½ x 11, paperback, illustrations

Alvyn Freed, Ph.D.
& Margaret Freed

ORDER NOW FOR 10% DISCOUNT ON 3 OR MORE TITLES.

T.A. FOR TEENS

Alvyn Freed, Ph.D.

TA for Teens (and other important people) (Gr. 8-12)

Over 100,000 sold. The book that tells teenagers they're OK! Provides help in growing into adulthood in a mixed-up world. Contrasts freedom and irresponsibility with knowing that youth need the skill, determination and *inner strength* to reach *fulfillment* and *self-esteem.* No talking down to kids.

0-915190-03-6, 258 pages, **JP-9003-6** **$18.95**
8½ x 11, paperback, illustrations

The Original Warm Fuzzy Tale (Gr. Pre K-12)

Over 100,000 sold. The concept of Warm Fuzzies and Cold Pricklies originated in this delightful story. A *fairy tale* in every sense, *with* adventure, fantasy, heroes, villians and a *moral*. Children (and adults, too) will enjoy this beautifully illustrated book. Great for parents and other care givers. **Songs of Warm Fuzzy Cass. $12.95**

0-915190-08-7, 48 pages, **JP-9008-7** **$7.95**
6 x 9, paperback, full color illustrations

Claude Steiner, Ph.D

ORDER FROM: B.L. Winch & Associates/Jalmar Press, 45 Hitching Post Drive, Bldg. 2, Rolling Hills Estates, CA 90274-5169
CALL TOLL FREE — (800) 662-9662. • (310) 547-1240. • FAX (310) 547-1644 • Add 10% shipping; $3 minimum

4/92

Order NOW 10% Discount On 3 Or More Titles!

20 YEARS
AWARD WINNING
PUBLISHER
P

OPEN your mind to wholebrain thinking and creative parenting.
GROW by leaps and bounds with our new ways to think and learn.

Openmind/Wholemind: Parenting and Teaching Tomorrow's Children Today (Staff/Personal)

Can we learn to *treat* the *brain/mind system* as *open* rather than closed? Can we learn to *use all* our *learning modalities*, *learning styles*, *creativities* and *intelligences* to create a product far greater than the sum of its parts? Yes! This primer for parents and teachers shows how.

Bob Samples, M.A.

0-915190-45-1, 272 pages, **JP-9045-1 $14.95**
7 x 10, paperback, 81 B/W photos, illust.

Unicorns Are Real: A Right-Brained Approach to Learning (Gr. K-Adult)

Over 100,000 sold. The *alternate methods of teaching/learning* developed by the author have helped literally thousands of children and adults with *learning difficulties*. A book of *simple ideas* and *activities* that are easy to use, yet dramatically effective. Video of techniques also available: VHS, 1½ hrs., JP-9113-0 $149.95. Unicorn Poster $4.95.

0-915190-35-4, 144 pages, **JP-9035-4 $12.95**
8½ x 11, paperback, illus., assessment

UNICORNS ARE REAL
A Right-Brained Approach to Learning

BARBARA MEISTER VITALE

Barbara Meister Vitale, M.A.

NOT JUST AUTHORS BUT RESEARCHERS AND PRACTITIONERS.

REVISED

THE
METAPHORIC
MIND
BOB SAMPLES

Metaphoric Mind: A Celebration of Creative Consciousness (Revised) (Staff/Personal)

A plea for a balanced way of thinking and being in a culture that stands on the knife-edge between *catastrophe* and *transformation*. The metaphoric mind is *asking* again, quietly but insistently, *for equilibrium*. For, after all, equilibrium is the way of nature. A revised version of a classic.

Bob Samples, M.A.

0-915190-68-0, 272 pages, **JP-9068-0 $16.95**
7 x 10, paperback, B/W photos, illus.

Free Flight: Celebrating Your Right Brain (Staff/Personal)

Journey with Barbara Meister Vitale, from her uncertain childhood perceptions of being *"different"* to the acceptance and adult celebration of that difference. A how to *book for right-brained people in a left-brained world.* Foreword by Bob Samples- *"This book is born of the human soul."* Great gift item for your right-brained friends.

0-915190-44-3, 128 pages, **JP-9044-3 $9.95**
5½ x 8½, paperback, illustrations

Free Flight

Barbara Meister Vitale, M.A.

NEW

IMAGINE THAT!

Imagine That! Getting Smarter Through Imagery Practice (Gr. K-Adult)

Understand and *develop* your own *seven intelligences* in only minutes a day. Help children do the same. The results will amaze you. Clear, step-by-step ways show you how to create your own imagery exercises for any area of learning or life and how to *relate imagery* exercises *to curriculum* content.

Lane Longino Waas, Ph.D.

0-915190-71-0, 144 pages, **JP-9071-0 $12.95**
6 x 9, paperback, 42 B/W photos, biblio.

Becoming Whole (Learning) Through Games (Gr. K-Adult)

New ideas for old games. *Develop* your *child's brain power, motivation* and *self-esteem* by playing. An excellent parent/ teacher guide and skills checklist to 100 standard games. Included are auditory, visual, motor, directional, modality, attention, educational, social and memory skills. Great resource for care givers.

0-915190-70-2, 288 pages, **JP-9070-2 $16.95**
6 x 9, paperback, glossary, biblio.

BECOMING WHOLE
Learning
THROUGH GAMES

NEW

Gwen Bailey Moore, Ph.D. & Todd Serby

100% TESTED — 100% PRACTICAL — 100% GUARANTEED.

Present Yourself!

By Michael J. Gelb

Present Yourself: Great Presentation Skills (Staff/Personal)

Use *mind mapping* to become a presenter who is a dynamic part of the message. Learn about transforming fear, knowing your audience, setting the stage, making them remember and much more. *Essential reading* for anyone interested in *communication*. This book will become the standard work in its field. **Hardback, JP-9050-8 $16.95**

Michael J. Gelb, M.A.

0-915190-51-6, 128 pages, **JP-9051-6 $9.95**
6 x 9, paperback,illus., mind maps

The Two Minute Lover (Staff/Personal)

With wit, wisdom and compassion, "The Two-Minute Lovers" and their proteges guide you through the steps of *building* and *maintaining* an *effective relationship in a fast-paced world.* They offer encouragement, inspiration and practical techniques for living happily in a relationship, even when outside pressures are enormous. Done like the "One Minute Manager."

0-915190-52-4, 112 pages, **JP-9052-4 $9.95**
6 x 9, paperback, illustrations

Building Successful Relationships
The
Two Minute
Lover
2-00
Asa Sparks, Ph.D.

Asa Sparks, Ph.D.

ORDER NOW FOR 10% DISCOUNT ON 3 OR MORE TITLES.

The Turbulent Teens: Understanding Helping, Surviving (Parents/Counselors)

Come to grips with the difficult issues of rules and the limits of parental tolerance, recognizing the necessity for *flexibility* that takes into consideration changes in the adolescent as well as the imperative *need for control*, agreed upon *expectations* and *accountability*. A must read! Useful in counseling situations.

James E. Gardner, Ph.D.

0-913091-01-4, 224 pages, **JP-9101-4 $8.95**
6 x 9, paperback, case histories

The Parent Book: Raising Emotionally Mature Children - Ages 3-15 (Parents)

Improve *positive bonding* with your child in five easy steps: *listen* to the feelings; *learn* the basic concern; *develop* an action plan; *confront* with support; *spend* 1 to 1 time. Ideas for helping in 4 *self-esteem* related areas: *awareness; relating; competence; integrity*. 69 sub-catagories. Learn what's missing and what to do about it.

0-915190-15-X, 208 pages, **JP-9015-X $9.95**
8½ x 11, paperback, illus., diag/Rx.

THE PARENT BOOK

Howard Besell, Ph.D. & Thomas P. Kelly, Jr.

ORDER FROM: B.L. Winch & Associates/Jalmar Press, 45 Hitching Post Drive, Bldg. 2, Rolling Hills Estates, CA 90274-5169
CALL TOLL FREE — (800) 662-9662. • (310) 547-1240 • FAX (310) 547-1644 • Add 10% shipping; $3 minimum